Teacher's Guide 4
Comprehension Skills

Author: Abigail Steel

William Collins' dream of knowledge for all began with the publication of his first book in 1819.

A self-educated mill worker, he not only enriched millions of lives, but also founded a flourishing publishing house. Today, staying true to this spirit, Collins books are packed with inspiration, innovation and practical expertise. They place you at the centre of a world of possibility and give you exactly what you need to explore it.

Collins. Freedom to teach.

Published by Collins
An imprint of HarperCollins*Publishers*
The News Building
1 London Bridge Street
London
SE1 9GF

Browse the complete Collins catalogue at
www.collins.co.uk

© HarperCollins*Publishers* Limited 2017

10 9 8 7 6 5 4 3 2 1

ISBN 978-0-00-822293-2

All rights reserved. No part of this publication may be reproduced, stored in a retrieval system, or transmitted in any form by any means, electronic, mechanical, photocopying, recording or otherwise, without the prior written permission of the Publisher or a licence permitting restricted copying in the United Kingdom issues by the Copyright Licensing Agency Ltd., 90 Tottenham Court Road, London W1T 4LP.

British Library Cataloguing in Publication Data

A catalogue record for this publication is available from the British Library.

Publishing Director: Lee Newman
Publishing Manager: Helen Doran
Senior Editor: Hannah Dove
Project Manager: Emily Hooton
Author: Abigail Steel
Development Editor: Hannah Hirst-Dunton
Copy-editor: Ros and Chris Davies
Proofreader: Gaynor Spry
Cover design and artwork: Amparo Barrera and Ken Vail Graphic Design
Internal design concept: Amparo Barrera
Typesetter: Jouve India Private Ltd
Illustrations: Alberto Saichann (Beehive Illustration)
Production Controller: Rachel Weaver

Printed and bound by CPI Group (UK) Ltd, Croydon, CR0 4YY

Acknowledgements

The publishers wish to thank the following for permission to reproduce content. Every effort has been made to trace copyright holders and to obtain their permission for the use of copyright materials. The publishers will gladly receive any information enabling them to rectify any error or omission at the first opportunity.

David Higham Associates Ltd for the poem on pages 24–25, 67 "I love our orange tent" by Berlie Doherty from *Story Chest: Big Bulgy Fat Black Slugs,* Thomas Nelson, 1993. Reproduced by permission of David Higham Associates Ltd; HarperCollins Publishers Ltd for extracts on page 83 from *In the Rue Bel Tesoro* by Lin Coghlan, copyright © 2011 Lin Coghlan. Reproduced by permission of HarperCollins Publishers Ltd; Tunji Beier for the poem on pages 45–46 "Kob Antelope" translated by Ulli Beier. Reproduced by kind permission; Andersen Press Ltd for extracts on pages 47–48, 89 from *Angry Arthur* by Hiawyn Oram, 1982. Reproduced with permission; and Wes Magee for the poem on pages 52–53 "What is ... The Sun?" from *The Witch's Brew and Other Poems* by Wes Magee, Cambridge University Press, 1989. Reproduced by permission of the author Wes Magee.

Contents

About Treasure House 4
Support, embed and challenge 12
Assessment 13
Support with teaching comprehension 14
Delivering the 2014 National Curriculum for English 16
Unit 1: Non-fiction (web page): Thrills City 22
Unit 2: Poetry: 'I Love Our Orange Tent' 24
Unit 3: Poetry: 'The Donkey' 26
Unit 4: Non-fiction (newspaper report): The Accident 28
Unit 5: Non-fiction (diary): Holiday diary 30
Unit 6: Fiction (fable): 'The Eagle and the Turtle' 32
Unit 7: Fiction (classic): 'Cockadoodle-Doo, Mr Sultana!' .. 34
Review unit 1: Fiction: 'Aladdin and the Genies' 36
Unit 8: Fiction (classic): 'The Wind in the Willows' 37
Unit 9: Fiction (historical): 'Stowaway!' 39
Unit 10: Playscript: 'In the Rue Bel Tesoro' 41
Unit 11: Fiction: 'The Day the Helicopters Came' 43
Unit 12: Poetry: Humans – Friends or Foes? 45
Unit 13: Fiction: 'Angry Arthur' and Poetry: 'My Hair as Black as Dirty Coal' 47
Unit 14: Non-fiction (information text): 'Feathered Record Breakers' 49
Review unit 2: Non-fiction (information text): 'Extreme Sports' 51
Unit 15: Non-fiction (information text): 'What is the Sun?' and Poetry: 'What is the Sun?' 52
Unit 16: Poetry: 'Whale Alert' 54
Unit 17: Fiction (modern): 'Cave Wars' 56
Unit 18: Playscript: 'Sophie's Rules' 58
Unit 19: Non-fiction (information text): 'Black Holes' 60
Unit 20: Fiction (modern): 'Tiger Dead! Tiger Dead!' 62
Review unit 3: Poetry: 'Feeding the Ducks' 64
Photocopiable resources 65

About Treasure House

Treasure House is a comprehensive and flexible bank of books and online resources for teaching the English curriculum. The Treasure House series offers two different pathways: one covering each English strand discretely (Skills Focus Pathway) and one integrating texts and the strands to create a programme of study (Integrated English Pathway). This Teacher's Guide is part of the Skills Focus Pathway.

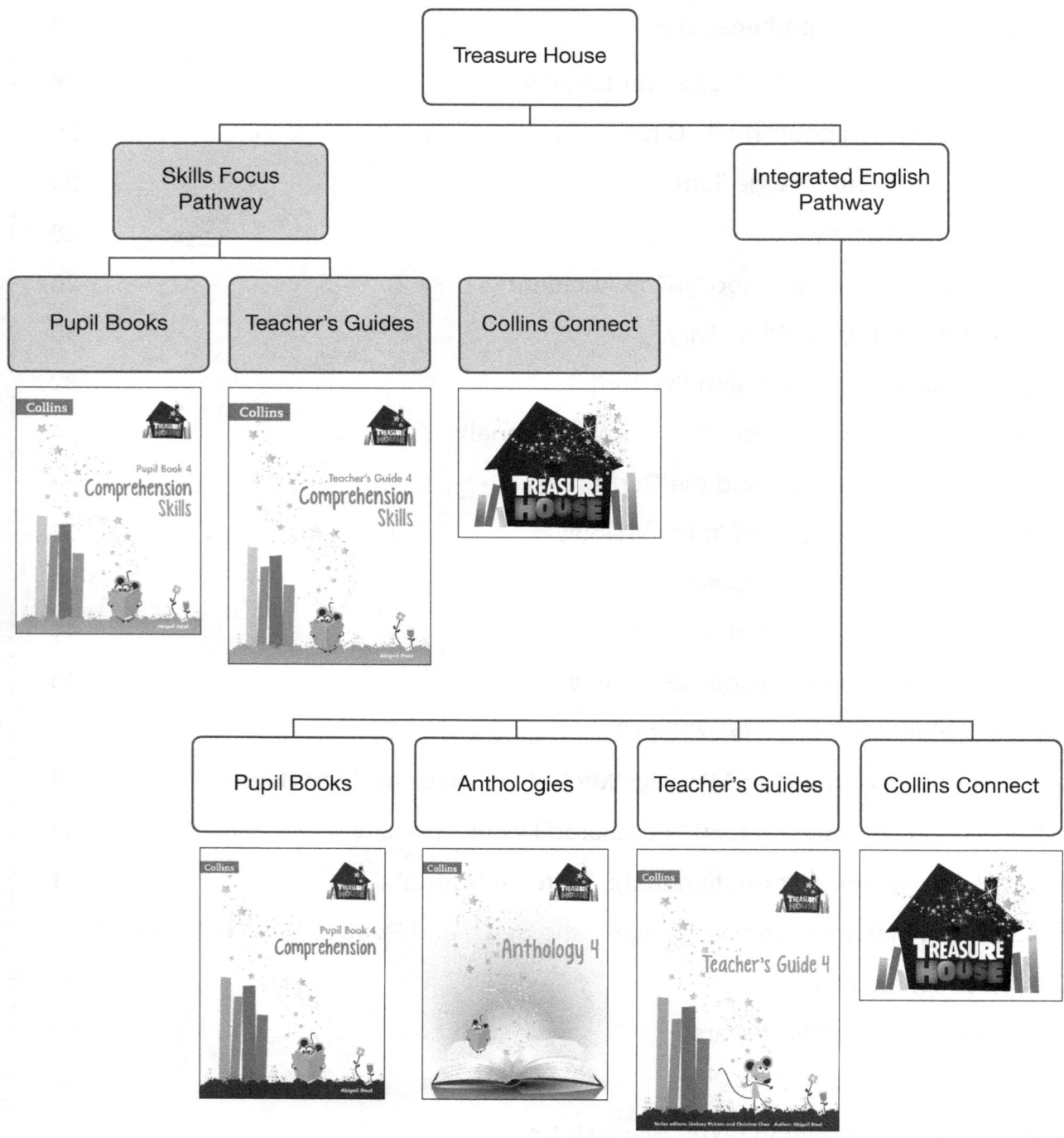

About Treasure House

1. Skills Focus

The Skills Focus Pupil Books and Teacher's Guides for all four strands (Comprehension; Spelling; Composition; and Vocabulary, Grammar and Punctuation) allow you to teach each curriculum area in a targeted way. Each unit in the Pupil Book is mapped directly to the statutory requirements of the National Curriculum. Each Teacher's Guide provides step-by-step instructions to guide you through the Pupil Book activities and digital Collins Connect resources for each competency. With a clear focus on skills and clearly-listed curriculum objectives you can select the appropriate resources to support your lessons.

2. Integrated English

Alternatively, the Integrated English pathway offers a complete programme of genre-based teaching sequences. There is one Teacher's Guide and one Anthology for each year group. Each Teacher's Guide provides 15 teaching sequences focused on different genres of text such as fairy tales, letters and newspaper articles. The Anthologies contain the classic texts, fiction, non-fiction and poetry required for each sequence. Each sequence also weaves together all four dimensions of the National Curriculum for English – Comprehension; Spelling; Composition; and Vocabulary, Grammar and Punctuation – into a complete English programme. The Pupil Books and Collins Connect provide targeted explanation of key points and practice activities organised by strand. This programme provides 30 weeks of teaching inspiration.

 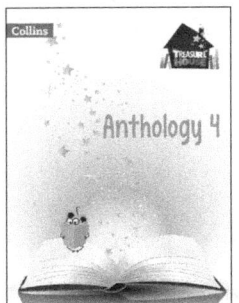  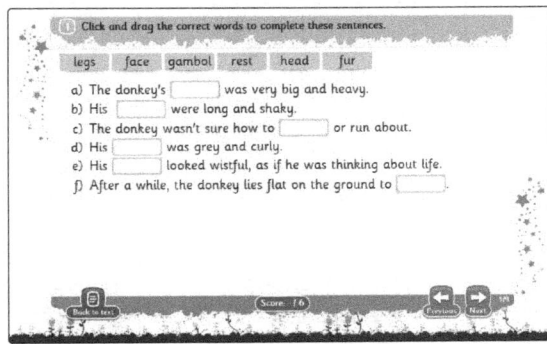

Other components

Handwriting Books, Handwriting Workbooks, Word Books and the online digital resources on Collins Connect are suitable for use with both pathways.

About Treasure House

Treasure House Skills Focus Teacher's Guides

Year	Comprehension	Composition	Vocabulary, Grammar and Punctuation	Spelling
1	978-0-00-822290-1	978-0-00-822302-1	978-0-00-822296-3	978-0-00-822308-3
2	978-0-00-822291-8	978-0-00-822303-8	978-0-00-822297-0	978-0-00-822309-0
3	978-0-00-822292-5	978-0-00-822304-5	978-0-00-822298-7	978-0-00-822310-6
4	978-0-00-822293-2	978-0-00-822305-2	978-0-00-822299-4	978-0-00-822311-3
5	978-0-00-822294-9	978-0-00-822306-9	978-0-00-822300-7	978-0-00-822312-0
6	978-0-00-822295-6	978-0-00-822307-6	978-0-00-822301-4	978-0-00-822313-7

About Treasure House

Inside the Skills Focus Teacher's Guides

The teaching notes in each unit in the Teacher's Guide provide you with subject information or background, a range of whole class and differentiated activities including photocopiable resource sheets and links to the Pupil Book and the online Collins Connect activities.

Each **Overview** provides clear objectives for each lesson tied into the new curriculum, links to the other relevant components and a list of any additional resources required.

Teaching overview provides a brief introduction to the specific skill concept or text type and some pointers on how to approach it.

Support, embed & challenge supports a mastery approach with activities provided at three levels.

Introduce the concept/text provides 5–10 minutes of preliminary discussion points or class/group activities to get the pupils engaged in the lesson focus and set out any essential prior learning.

Pupil practice gives guidance and the answers to each of the three sections in the Pupil Book: *Get started*, *Try these* and *Now try these*.

Homework / Additional activities lists ideas for classroom or homework activities, and relevant activities from Collins Connect.

Two photocopiable **resource** worksheets per unit provide extra practice of the specific lesson concept. They are designed to be used with the activities in support, embed or challenge sections.

About Treasure House

Treasure House Skills Focus Pupil Books

There are four Skills Focus Pupil Books for each year group, based on the four dimensions of the National Curriculum for English: Comprehension; Spelling; Composition; and Vocabulary, Grammar and Punctuation. The Pupil Books provide a child-friendly introduction to each subject and a range of initial activities for independent pupil-led learning. A Review unit for each term assesses pupils' progress.

Year	Comprehension	Composition	Vocabulary, Grammar and Punctuation	Spelling
1	978-0-00-823634-2	978-0-00-823646-5	978-0-00-823640-3	978-0-00-823652-6
2	978-0-00-823635-9	978-0-00-823647-2	978-0-00-823641-0	978-0-00-823653-3
3	978-0-00-823636-6	978-0-00-823648-9	978-0-00-823642-7	978-0-00-823654-0
4	978-0-00-823637-3	978-0-00-823649-6	978-0-00-823643-4	978-0-00-823655-7
5	978-0-00-823638-0	978-0-00-823650-2	978-0-00-823644-1	978-0-00-823656-4
6	978-0-00-823639-7	978-0-00-823651-9	978-0-00-823645-8	978-0-00-823657-1

About Treasure House

Inside the Skills Focus Pupil Books
Comprehension

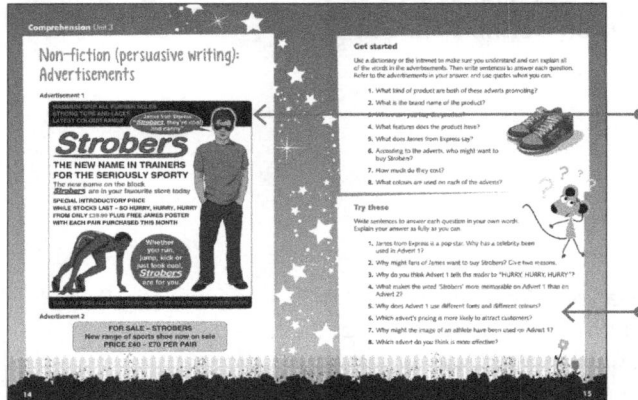

Includes high-quality text extracts covering poetry, prose, traditional tales, playscripts and non-fiction.

Pupils retrieve and record information, learn to draw inferences from texts and increase their familiarity with a wide range of literary genres.

Composition

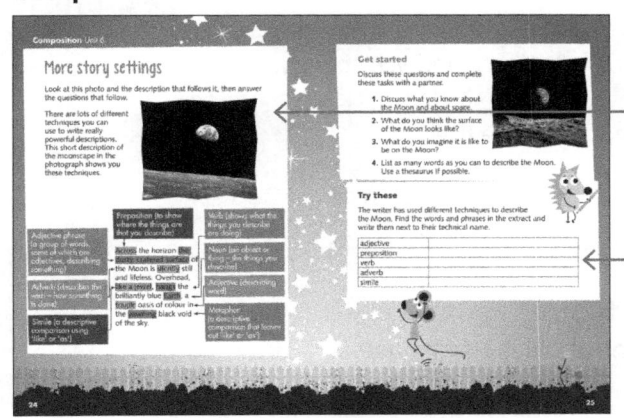

Includes high-quality, annotated text extracts as models for different types of writing.

Children learn how to write effectively and for a purpose.

Vocabulary, Grammar and Punctuation

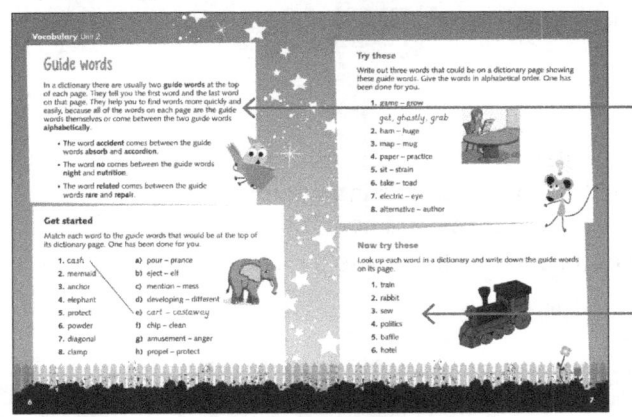

Develops children's knowledge and understanding of grammar and punctuation skills.

A rule is introduced and explained. Children are given lots of opportunities to practise using it.

Spelling

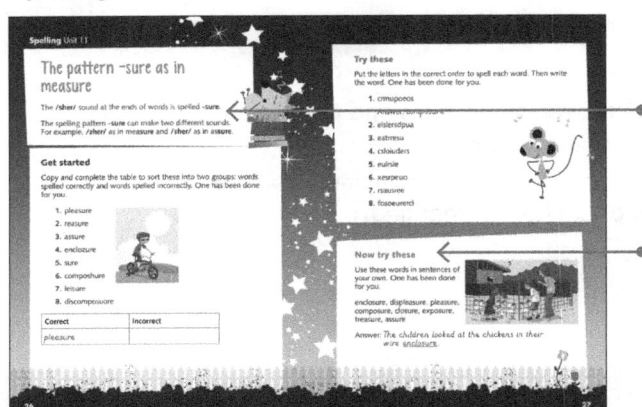

Spelling rules are introduced and explained.

Practice is provided for spotting and using the spelling rules, correcting misspelt words and using the words in context.

About Treasure House

Treasure House on Collins Connect

Digital resources for Treasure House are available on Collins Connect which provides a wealth of interactive activities. Treasure House is organised into six core areas on Collins Connect:

- Comprehension
- Spelling
- Composition
- Vocabulary, Grammar and Punctuation
- The Reading Attic
- Teacher's Guides and Anthologies.

For most units in the Skills Focus Pupil Books, there is an accompanying Collins Connect unit focused on the same teaching objective. These fun, independent activities can be used for initial pupil-led learning, or for further practice using a different learning environment. Either way, with Collins Connect, you have a wealth of questions to help children embed their learning.

Treasure House on Collins Connect is available via subscription at connect.collins.co.uk

Features of Treasure House on Collins Connect

The digital resources enhance children's comprehension, spelling, composition, and vocabulary, grammar, punctuation skills through providing:

- a bank of varied and engaging interactive activities so children can practise their skills independently
- audio support to help children access the texts and activities
- auto-mark functionality so children receive instant feedback and have the opportunity to repeat tasks.

Teachers benefit from useful resources and time-saving tools including:

- teacher-facing materials such as audio and explanations for front-of-class teaching or pupil-led learning
- lesson starter videos for some Composition units
- downloadable teaching notes for all online activities
- downloadable teaching notes for Skills Focus and Integrated English pathways
- the option to assign homework activities to your classes
- class records to monitor progress.

Comprehension

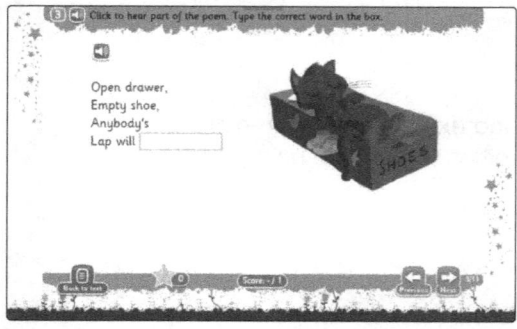

- Includes high-quality text extracts covering poetry, prose, traditional tales, playscripts and non-fiction.
- Audio function supports children to access the text and the activities

Composition

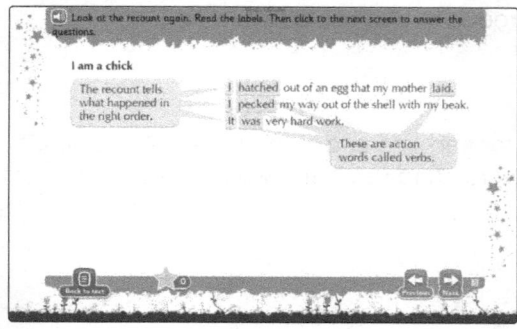

- Activities support children to develop and build more sophisticated sentence structures.
- Every unit ends with a longer piece of writing that can be submitted to the teacher for marking.

About Treasure House

Vocabulary, Grammar and Punctuation

- Fun, practical activities develop children's knowledge and understanding of grammar and punctuation skills.
- Each skill is reinforced with a huge, varied bank of practice questions.

Spelling

- Fun, practical activities develop children's knowledge and understanding of each spelling rule.
- Each rule is reinforced with a huge, varied bank of practice questions.
- Children spell words using an audio prompt, write their own sentences and practise spelling using Look Say Cover Write Check.

Reading Attic

- Children's love of reading is nurtured with texts from exciting children's authors including Micheal Bond, David Walliams and Micheal Morpurgo.
- Lesson sequences accompany the texts, with drama opportunities and creative strategies for engaging children with key themes, characters and plots.
- Whole-book projects encourage reading for pleasure.

Treasure House Digital Teacher's Guides and Anthologies

The teaching sequences and anthology texts for each year group are included as a flexible bank of resources.

The teaching notes for each skill strand and year group are also included on Collins Connect.

Support, embed and challenge

Treasure House provides comprehensive, detailed differentiation at three levels to ensure that all children are able to access achievement. It is important that children master the basic skills before they go further in their learning. Children may make progress towards the standard at different speeds, with some not reaching it until the very end of the year.

In the Teacher's Guide, Support, Embed and Challenge sections allow teachers to keep the whole class focussed with no child left behind. Two photocopiable resources per unit offer additional material linked to the Support, Embed or Challenge sections.

Support

The Support section offers simpler or more scaffolded activities that will help learners who have not yet grasped specific concepts covered. Background information may also be provided to help children to contextualise learning. This enables children to make progress so that they can keep up with the class.

To help with reading comprehension, some support activities help learners to access the core text, for example, by giving some background information to the story or support with figurative speech. This is more motivating and enjoyable than offering a simplified text.

If you have a teaching assistant, you may wish to ask him or her to help children work through these activities. You might then ask children who have completed these activities to progress to other more challenging tasks found in the Embed or Challenge sections – or you may decide more practice of the basics is required. Collins Connect can provide further activities.

Embed

The Embed section includes activities to embed learning and is aimed at those who children who are working at the expected standard. It ensures that learners have understood key teaching objectives for the age-group. These activities could be used by the whole class or groups, and most are appropriate for both teacher-led and independent work.

In Comprehension, all children should cross the threshold of reading the texts in Treasure House; however, the depth of their analysis and understanding will vary depending on prior experience, current interests and motivation. Activities in the Embed section encourage children to apply their learning by further analysing the text or by planning their own writing based on the same theme or text-type.

Challenge

The Challenge section provides additional tasks, questions or activities that will push children who have mastered the concept without difficulty. This keeps children motivated and allows them to gain a greater depth of understanding. You may wish to give these activities to fast finishers to work through independently.

In Comprehension, children explore the text-type or theme further through drama, research, discussion or by doing their own writing.

Assessment

Teacher's Guides
There are opportunities for assessment throughout the Treasure House series. The teaching notes in Treasure House Teacher's Guides offer ideas for questions, informal assessment and spelling tests.

Pupil Book Review units
Each Pupil Book has three Review units designed as a quick formative assessment tool for the end of each term. Questions assess the work that has been covered over the previous units. These review units will provide you with an informal way of measuring your pupils' progress. You may wish to use these as Assessment for Learning to help you and your pupils to understand where they are in their learning journey.

The Review units in the Comprehension Pupil Books provide children with a new text or extract to read and understand. Children can draw on what they have learned during the term to help them access the new text without an initial teaching session to guide them. Questions types may reoccur across the Review units allowing you to see progression across the year, and the three reviews will always cover all three genres: fiction, non-fiction and poetry.

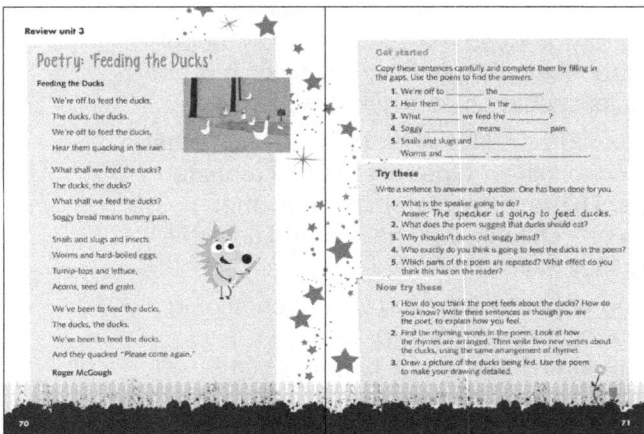

Assessment in Collins Connect
Activities on Collins Connect can also be used for effective assessment. Activities with auto-marking mean that if children answer incorrectly, they can make another attempt helping them to analyse their own work for mistakes. Homework activities can also be assigned to classes through Collins Connect. At the end of activities, children can select a smiley face to indicate how they found the task giving you useful feedback on any gaps in knowledge.

Class records on Collins Connect allow you to get an overview of children's progress with several features. You can choose to view records by unit, pupil or strand. By viewing detailed scores, you can view pupils' scores question by question in a clear table-format to help you establish areas where there might be particular strengths and weaknesses both class-wide and for individuals.

If you wish, you can also set mastery judgements (mastery achieved and exceeded, mastery achieved, mastery not yet achieved) to help see where your children need more help.

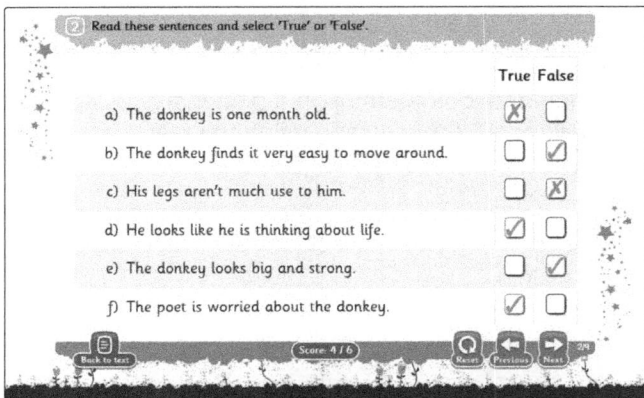

Support with teaching comprehension

The teacher's guides for Comprehension units can be followed in a simple linear fashion that structures the lesson into five sections:

- assessment of existing skills and knowledge, and an introduction to the unit's source text
- reading the source text
- completion of the 'pupil practice' questions
- differentiated work, following the Support, Embed and Challenge activity guidance (using the provided photocopiable worksheets)
- homework or additional activities.

However, this lesson structure is intended to be flexible. While we recommend that the first three of these steps should usually be followed in the given order, work following the pupil practice questions can be manipulated in numerous ways to suit the needs, skills and preferences of your class.

For example, you may wish to set one of the differentiation activities as homework for the whole class, or to guide children through an 'additional' activity during the lesson, rather than setting it as homework. You may alternatively judge that your class has firmly grasped the concept being taught, and choose not to use any activity suggested, or perhaps introduce only the Extend activity: it is not essential that every activity outlined in the teacher's guide units should be completed.

With the same motivation, many activities (and worksheets) could be adapted for reuse in units other than the one for which they are provided. Several activity and worksheet types are already repeated in similar forms between (and sometimes within) year groups. This is in order both to show the children's changing levels of attainment directly, and to allow any children who have found an activity challenging to reattempt it in a new context after developing their skills.

If, however, children find a particular activity either challenging or particularly engaging, you should also feel free to repeat that activity, where appropriate, at your own discretion. For example, if children enjoy considering appropriate costumes and settings when looking at a playscript (an activity, with worksheet, suggested in Year 3 Unit 17), this activity could be adapted to fit any playscript source text – and many prose fiction texts, too.

You may also wish to consider using Support activities in conjunction with the pupil practice questions, if children are struggling with content or a concept with which the Support activity deals. For example, if questions within the 'Try these' and 'Now try these' sections of pupil practice require understanding of similes, you may wish to intervene and prepare children using an appropriate Support activity (such as suggested in Year 3 Unit 2).

By using the teacher's guide units and their suggested activities flexibly, you can choose to tailor the resources at your fingertips to provide the most beneficial learning system for the children being taught.

Teaching comprehension is a key part of achieving the universal aim of developing children's love of literature through widespread reading for enjoyment. If children are confident and fluent readers, who understand the form and content of the texts they read they are more likely to enjoy them.

We can make learning comprehension easy and fun by employing simple techniques to guide children along their reading journey.

Modelling

When reading a letter or newspaper article to the class remember to hesitate on words that they might not know, intimate that you are unsure of the proper meaning and look them up in a dictionary. You might also model how you use context or grammar clues to work out the meaning using the rest of the text.

Support with teaching comprehension

Making predictions

When embarking on any new text ask children to consider what they think it will be about, or what they think might happen. Show how to look for clues in the presentation of the text or the introductory information you have. Remember to model making your own predictions too – this gives you an opportunity to demonstrate how to rationalize a prediction by speaking your thought processes aloud.

Questioning

Questioning can take many forms and penetrate many depths of understanding. Questions can be closed, requiring short, defined answers or they can be open, enabling the children to explore wider thoughts. Sometimes the best questions are those that are spontaneous and form part of a natural conversation exploring a text. Encourage children to form their own questions about the purpose, structure and content of texts – they could note these down and return to them later to see if they have discovered the answers after reading.

Retelling and summarizing

Encourage children to reflect upon what has happened in a text – this can be a surprisingly challenging activity. Provide plenty of demonstrations of how to retell and summarize. Retelling and summarizing can take many fun, interactive forms such as role play, radio presentations, creating news flash articles, and oral story retellings. Some children struggle with sequencing and ordering so build this in with your retelling activities.

Visualizing

When we read we create mental images of what is happening. Descriptions of people, places and action are acted out in our minds. For children this skill doesn't always come naturally. Ask children to close their eyes and focus on imagining how something looks. Compare written texts to the films and TV shows they are familiar with watching. Point out specific adjectives and adverbs that are actively working within the text to assist the reader. Enable children the opportunity to draw and paint their interpretations of the texts they read.

Connections to children's own experiences

Younger children are often better at pointing at when they recognise a similarity between their own life and something they read in a text. Older children tend to become less inward looking and aren't so forthcoming with the links they make to texts. Encourage them by asking direct questions: *Does anyone else recognise this event? Do you know a character like this? Have you ever been to a similar place? When have you felt that emotion like the character?* Making explicit connections with the text can advance children's understanding of not only the event being described but also the history to the event and the character's emotions. They are able to talk about the 'bigger picture'.

Delivering the 2014 National Curriculum for English

English Programme of Study	Units																			
Reading – comprehension	1	2	3	4	5	6	7	8	9	10	11	12	13	14	15	16	17	18	19	20
Develop positive attitudes to reading and understanding of what they read by:																				
Listening to and discussing a wide range of fiction, poetry, plays, non-fiction and reference books or textbooks	✓	✓	✓	✓	✓	✓	✓	✓	✓	✓	✓	✓	✓	✓	✓	✓	✓	✓	✓	✓
Reading books that are structured in different ways and reading for a range of purposes	✓	✓	✓	✓	✓	✓	✓	✓	✓	✓	✓	✓	✓	✓	✓	✓	✓	✓	✓	✓
Using dictionaries to check the meaning of words that they have read	✓	✓	✓	✓	✓	✓	✓	✓	✓	✓	✓	✓	✓	✓	✓	✓	✓	✓	✓	✓
Increasing their familiarity with a wide range of books, including fairy stories, myths and legends, and retelling some of these orally						✓	✓	✓		✓	✓		✓				✓	✓		✓
Identifying themes and conventions in a wide range of books	✓	✓	✓	✓	✓	✓	✓		✓	✓	✓	✓	✓	✓	✓	✓	✓	✓	✓	✓
Preparing poems and play scripts to read aloud and to perform, showing understanding through intonation, tone, volume and action			✓													✓		✓		
Discussing words and phrases that capture the reader's interest and imagination	✓	✓	✓	✓	✓	✓	✓	✓	✓		✓	✓	✓	✓	✓	✓	✓	✓	✓	✓
Recognising some different forms of poetry [for example, free verse, narrative poetry]		✓	✓													✓				

Understand what they read, in books they can read independently, by:	Checking that the text makes sense to them, discussing their understanding and explaining the meaning of words in context	✓	✓	✓	✓	✓	✓	✓	✓	✓	✓	✓	✓	✓	✓	✓	✓
	Asking questions to improve their understanding of a text	✓	✓	✓	✓	✓	✓	✓	✓	✓	✓	✓	✓	✓	✓		✓
	Drawing inferences such as inferring characters' feelings, thoughts and motives from their actions, and justifying inferences with evidence	✓	✓		✓	✓	✓	✓	✓	✓	✓	✓	✓				✓
	Predicting what might happen from details stated and implied			✓	✓	✓	✓	✓	✓	✓	✓		✓	✓			✓
	Identifying main ideas drawn from more than one paragraph and summarising these	✓		✓	✓	✓	✓	✓	✓	✓	✓	✓	✓	✓	✓	✓	✓
	Identifying how language, structure, and presentation contribute to meaning	✓	✓	✓	✓	✓	✓	✓	✓	✓	✓	✓	✓	✓	✓	✓	✓
Retrieve and record information from non-fiction		✓	✓	✓	✓	✓	✓	✓	✓	✓	✓	✓	✓		✓		
Participate in discussion about both books that are read to them and those they can read for themselves, taking turns and listening to what others say.		✓	✓	✓	✓	✓	✓	✓	✓	✓	✓	✓	✓	✓	✓	✓	✓

Treasure House resources overview

Unit	Title	Treasure House Resources	Collins Connect

1	Non-fiction (web page): Thrills City	• Comprehension Skills Pupil Book 4, Unit 1, pages 4–6
		• Comprehension Skills Teacher's Guide 4
		  – Unit 1, pages 22–23
		  – Photocopiable Unit 1, Resource 1: Plan a visit, page 65
		  – Photocopiable Unit 1, Resource 2: Design a website, page 66
			Collins Connect Treasure House Comprehension Year 4, Unit 1

2	Poetry: 'I Love Our Orange Tent'	• Comprehension Skills Pupil Book 4, Unit 2, pages 7–9
		• Comprehension Skills Teacher's Guide 4
		  – Unit 2, pages 24–25
		  – Photocopiable Unit 2, Resource 1: Similes, page 67
		  – Photocopiable Unit 2, Resource 2: My descriptive poem, page 68
			Collins Connect Treasure House Comprehension Year 4, Unit 2

3	Poetry: 'The Donkey'	• Comprehension Skills Pupil Book 4, Unit 3, pages 10–12
		• Comprehension Skills Teacher's Guide 4
		  – Unit 3, pages 26–27
		  – Photocopiable Unit 3, Resource 1: Comparing animals, page 69
		  – Photocopiable Unit 3, Resource 2: My new-born animal poem, page 70
			Collins Connect Treasure House Comprehension Year 4, Unit 3

4	Non-fiction (newspaper report): The Accident	• Comprehension Skills Pupil Book 4, Unit 4, pages 13–15
		• Comprehension Skills Teacher's Guide 4
		  – Unit 4, pages 28–29
		  – Photocopiable Unit 4, Resource 1: Find the facts, page 71
		  – Photocopiable Unit 4, Resource 2: Tell the story, page 72
			Collins Connect Treasure House Comprehension Year 4, Unit 4

5	Non-fiction (diary): Holiday diary	• Comprehension Skills Pupil Book 4, Unit 5, pages 16–18
		• Comprehension Skills Teacher's Guide 4
		  – Unit 5, pages 30–31
		  – Photocopiable Unit 5, Resource 1: A letter from the pilot, page 73
		  – Photocopiable Unit 5, Resource 2: A news report, page 74
			Collins Connect Treasure House Comprehension Year 4, Unit 5

6	Fiction (fable): 'The Eagle and the Turtle'	• Comprehension Skills Pupil Book 4, Unit 6, pages 19–21
		• Comprehension Skills Teacher's Guide 4
		  – Unit 6, pages 32–33
		  – Photocopiable Unit 6, Resource 1: Making decisions, page 75
		  – Photocopiable Unit 6, Resource 2: A story of advice, page 76
			Collins Connect Treasure House Comprehension Year 4, Unit 6

Unit	Title	Treasure House Resources	Collins Connect

7	Fiction (classic): 'Cockadoodle-Doo, Mr Sultana!'	• Comprehension Skills Pupil Book 4, Unit 7, pages 22–24
		• Comprehension Skills Teacher's Guide 4
		  – Unit 7, pages 34–35
		  – Photocopiable Unit 7, Resource 1: Before and after, page 77
		  – Photocopiable Unit 7, Resource 2: Finders keepers! page 78
			Collins Connect Treasure House Comprehension Year 4, Unit 7

8	Fiction (classic): 'The Wind in the Willows'	• Comprehension Skills Pupil Book 4, Unit 8, pages 28–30
		• Comprehension Skills Teacher's Guide 4
		  – Unit 8, pages 37–38
		  – Photocopiable Unit 8, Resource 1: Asking questions, page 79
		  – Photocopiable Unit 8, Resource 2: The next adventure, page 80
			Collins Connect Treasure House Comprehension Year 4, Unit 8

9	Fiction (historical): 'Stowaway!'	• Comprehension Skills Pupil Book 4, Unit 9, pages 31–33
		• Comprehension Skills Teacher's Guide 4
		  – Unit 9, pages 39–40
		  – Photocopiable Unit 9, Resource 1: Dickon's character, page 81
		  – Photocopiable Unit 9, Resource 2: A story starts, page 82
			Collins Connect Treasure House Comprehension Year 4, Unit 9

10	Playscript: 'In the Rue Bel Tesoro'	• Comprehension Skills Pupil Book 4, Unit 10, pages 34–36
		• Comprehension Skills Teacher's Guide 4
		  – Unit 10, pages 41–42
		  – Photocopiable Unit 10, Resource 1: Finding the features, page 83
		  – Photocopiable Unit 10, Resource 2: Costumes and setting, page 84
			Collins Connect Treasure House Comprehension Year 4, Unit 10

11	Fiction: 'The Day the Helicopters Came'	• Comprehension Skills Pupil Book 4, Unit 11, pages 37–39
		• Comprehension Skills Teacher's Guide 4
		  – Unit 11, pages 43–44
		  – Photocopiable Unit 11, Resource 1: The Vietnam War, page 85
		  – Photocopiable Unit 11, Resource 2: Character perspectives, page 86
			Collins Connect Treasure House Comprehension Year 4, Unit 11

12	Poetry: Humans – Friends or Foes?	• Comprehension Skills Pupil Book 4, Unit 12, pages 40–42
		• Comprehension Skills Teacher's Guide 4
		  – Unit 12, pages 45–46
		  – Photocopiable Unit 12, Resource 1: Describing the painting, page 87
		  – Photocopiable Unit 12, Resource 2: Making comparisons, page 88
			Collins Connect Treasure House Comprehension Year 4, Unit 12

Unit	Title	Treasure House Resources	Collins Connect

13	Fiction: 'Angry Arthur' and Poetry: 'My Hair as Black as Dirty Coal'	• Comprehension Skills Pupil Book 4, Unit 13, pages 43–45
		• Comprehension Skills Teacher's Guide 4
		  – Unit 13, pages 47–48
		  – Photocopiable Unit 13, Resource 1: Simile or metaphor? page 89
		  – Photocopiable Unit 13, Resource 2: Feeling angry, page 90
			Collins Connect Treasure House Comprehension Year 4, Unit 13

14	Non-fiction (information text): 'Feathered Record Breakers'	• Comprehension Skills Pupil Book 4, Unit 14, pages 46–48
		• Comprehension Skills Teacher's Guide 4
		  – Unit 14, pages 49–50
		  – Photocopiable Unit 14, Resource 1: True or false? page 91
		  – Photocopiable Unit 14, Resource 2: Bird fact file, page 92
			Collins Connect Treasure House Comprehension Year 4, Unit 14

15	Non-fiction (information text): 'What is the Sun?' and Poetry: 'What is the Sun?'	• Comprehension Skills Pupil Book 4, Unit 15, pages 52–54
		• Comprehension Skills Teacher's Guide 4
		  – Unit 15, pages 52–53
		  – Photocopiable Unit 15, Resource 1: The sun, page 93
		  – Photocopiable Unit 15, Resource 2: The moon, page 94
			Collins Connect Treasure House Comprehension Year 4, Unit 15

16	Poetry: 'Whale Alert'	• Comprehension Skills Pupil Book 4, Unit 16, pages 55–57
		• Comprehension Skills Teacher's Guide 4
		  – Unit 16, pages 54–55
		  – Photocopiable Unit 16, Resource 1: Whale fact file, page 95
		  – Photocopiable Unit 16, Resource 2: A letter to whale hunters, page 96	

17	Fiction (modern): 'Cave Wars'	• Comprehension Skills Pupil Book 4, Unit 17, pages 58–60
		• Comprehension Skills Teacher's Guide 4
		  – Unit 17, pages 56–57
		  – Photocopiable Unit 17, Resource 1: Now and then, page 97
		  – Photocopiable Unit 17, Resource 2: Us and them, page 98	

18	Playscript: 'Sophie's Rules'	• Comprehension Skills Pupil Book 4, Unit 18, pages 61–63
		• Comprehension Skills Teacher's Guide 4
		  – Unit 18, pages 58–59
		  – Photocopiable Unit 18, Resource 1: Sophie and Dana, page 99
		  – Photocopiable Unit 18, Resource 2: Different characters, page 100	

Unit	Title	Treasure House Resources	Collins Connect

19	Non-fiction (information text): 'Black Holes'	• Comprehension Skills Pupil Book 4, Unit 19, pages 64–66
		• Comprehension Skills Teacher's Guide 4
		  – Unit 19, pages 60–61
		  – Photocopiable Unit 19, Resource 1: True or false? page 101
		  – Photocopiable Unit 19, Resource 2: Once upon a time, in space…, page 102	

20	Fiction (modern): 'Tiger Dead! Tiger Dead!'	• Comprehension Skills Pupil Book 4, Unit 20, pages 67–69
		• Comprehension Skills Teacher's Guide 4
		  – Unit 20, pages 62–63
		  – Photocopiable Unit 20, Resource 1: Tiger's plan, page 103
		  – Photocopiable Unit 20, Resource 2: Anansi's plan, page 104	

Unit 1: Non-fiction (web page): Thrills City

Overview

English curriculum objectives

- Listen to and discuss a wide range of fiction, poetry, plays, non-fiction and reference books or textbooks
- Read books that are structured in different ways and reading for a range of purposes
- Use dictionaries to check the meanings of words they have read
- Identify themes and conventions in a wide range of books
- Discuss words and phrases that capture the reader's interest and imagination
- Check that the text makes sense to them, discussing their understanding and explaining the meaning of words in context
- Ask questions to improve their understanding of a text
- Draw inferences such as inferring characters' feelings, thoughts and motives from their actions, and justifying inferences with evidence
- Identify main ideas drawn from more than one paragraph and summarise these
- Identify how language, structure and presentation contribute to meaning
- Retrieve and record information from non-fiction
- Participate in discussion about both books that are read to them and those they can read for themselves, taking turns and listening to what others say

Treasure House resources

- Comprehension Skills Pupil Book 4, Unit 1, pages 4–6
- Collins Connect Treasure House Comprehension Year 4, Unit 1
- Photocopiable Unit 1, Resource 1: Plan a visit, page 65
- Photocopiable Unit 1, Resource 2: Design a website, page 66

Additional resources

- Dictionaries or the internet (optional)
- Access to real theme park websites (optional)

Introduction

Teaching overview

Thrills City is an example of a website advertising, and giving information about, a (fictional) theme park. It features characteristics such as headings, subheadings, menu tabs, bullet points, special offers and an email sign-up box. The information on the web page enables a reader to plan a visit, and to think about activities they might enjoy doing at the park.

Introduce the text

Ask the children if any of them has been to a theme park. If they have, invite them to share their experiences with the class. Then ask them if they know why a theme park or activity centre might have a website. Take suggestions, and establish that a website could help future visitors by providing information that will help them plan their trip, and show them what they can enjoy there.

Tell the children that, in this lesson, they will focus on an image depicting a website home page for a theme park. Then they will answer questions about it. Remind children that sometimes the answers to the questions will be clearly written in the text, but that sometimes they may need to think a little harder and use their own ideas, supported by the text.

Ask the children to read the text individually or in pairs. Ask them to note down any words they do not understand. Discuss unknown or unusual vocabulary before setting children to work answering the questions in the Pupil Book. Try to avoid discussing the content of the text until after the children have answered the questions.

Pupil practice

Get started

Children copy the sentences and complete them using information from the text.

Answers

1. Thrills City has a club for younger guests called the <u>Over the Rainbow Club</u>. [1 mark]

Pupil Book pages 4–6

2. Guests might want to relax in the spa and <u>health club</u>. [1 mark]
3. You can have fun swimming in the <u>water park</u>. [1 mark]
4. If you sign up now for information and offers to be sent by email, you will become a <u>Select Guest</u>. [1 mark]

22

Unit 1: Non-fiction (web page): Thrills City

5. You can watch live entertainment and meet characters. [1 mark]

Try these

Assist children if they ask for help with vocabulary, first discussing what they think the words might mean. Ask children to write sentences to answer the questions, explaining their answers with reference to the text and their own experiences.

Suggested answers

1. *I would click on the 'What's on' button to learn more about events happening at Thrills City.* [example]

2. You could save money on tickets for a trip in June by buying 2-for-1 tickets and by printing your tickets at home. [2 marks]

3. Yes, you could visit the park on a Sunday. I know this because the web page says 'Open 10 a.m. to 6 p.m. every day'. [1 mark]

4. Yes, you could get something to eat there. I think this because there is a pink button labelled 'Restaurants'. [1 mark]

5. Driving would be a good way to get there. I think this because the web page says 'Close to motorway' and 'Free parking'. [1 mark]

Now try these
Open-ended questions

1. Questions should be from a future visitor's point of view, and children should make educated guesses about where on the website they might be answered (that is, on the 'About', 'Plan a visit', 'What's on', 'Our rides' or 'Restaurants' web page). [3 marks max]

2. Accept any well-structured web page (probably resembling that constituting the extract) that provides information relevant for planning a visit to Thrills City. Details could include how to get there, where to park, where to collect tickets, ideas for what to do first, different lengths and times of routes around the park and helpful information such as where toilets or different rides are. [3 marks max]

3. The information on the leaflets should be useful and clear. All information on the extract home page should be included. [3 marks max]

Support, embed & challenge

Support
Use Unit 1 Resource 1: Plan a visit to support children in paying close attention to the detail of the website extract, as well as thinking about how to use the information in a real-life context. Ask children to use the worksheet to plan a visit to the theme park suitable for a large family group.

Embed
Use Unit 1 Resource 2: Design a website to encourage children to apply their understanding of a website's layout by creating their own website design using the template. Remind children to think about the information their users may want to find, and to include the tabs they will need to take their users to different web pages.

Challenge
Challenge children to think about the information displayed on other websites, such as a retail or sports club home page. Ask them to compare how the websites are similar and different. Ask: 'What do you think makes a website successful?'

Homework / Additional activities

Real-life websites
Ask children to research and find a website for a local theme park or activity centre. Ask them to make notes on the features that it has. Ask: 'How is the website similar to and different from the website studied in the lesson?'

Collins Connect: Unit 1
Ask the children to complete Unit 1 (see Teach → Year 4 → Comprehension → Unit 1).

Unit 2: Poetry: 'I Love Our Orange Tent'

Overview

English curriculum objectives

- Listen to and discuss a wide range of fiction, poetry, plays, non-fiction and reference books or textbooks
- Read books that are structured in different ways and reading for a range of purposes
- Use dictionaries to check the meanings of words they have read
- Identify themes and conventions in a wide range of books
- Prepare poems and playscripts to read aloud and to perform, showing understanding through intonation, tone, volume and action
- Discuss words and phrases that capture the reader's interest and imagination
- Recognise some different forms of poetry
- Check that the text makes sense to them, discussing their understanding and explaining the meaning of words in context
- Ask questions to improve their understanding of a text
- Draw inferences such as inferring characters' feelings, thoughts and motives from their actions, and justifying inferences with evidence
- Identify how language, structure and presentation contribute to meaning
- Participate in discussion about both books that are read to them and those they can read for themselves, taking turns and listening to what others say

Treasure House resources

- Comprehension Skills Pupil Book 4, Unit 2, pages 7–9
- Collins Connect Treasure House Comprehension Year 4, Unit 2
- Photocopiable Unit 2, Resource 1: Similes, page 67
- Photocopiable Unit 2, Resource 2: My descriptive poem, page 68

Additional resources

- Dictionaries or the internet (optional)
- Other highly descriptive poems (optional)

Introduction

Teaching overview

'I Love Our Orange Tent' is a poem that vividly describes a child's senses and feelings in connection with their tent. The poem contains examples of similes and is in blank verse: it has no formal rhyme structure.

Introduce the poem

Ask the children if they have ever been camping in a tent. If they have, invite them to share their experiences with the class. Then ask them what they think makes something a poem. Discuss the children's opinions, and ensure that you point out that not all poems rhyme.

Tell the children that, in this lesson, they will focus on a poem that gives vivid descriptions of the speaker's feelings about their tent. Then they will answer questions about it. Remind children that sometimes the answers to the questions will be clearly written in the poem, but that sometimes they may need to think a little harder and use their own ideas, supported by the text.

Ask the children to read the poem individually or in pairs. Ask them to note down any words they do not understand. Discuss unknown or unusual vocabulary before setting children to work answering the questions in the Pupil Book. Try to avoid discussing the content of the poem until after the children have answered the questions.

Pupil practice

Pupil Book pages 7–9

Get started

Children copy the sentences and complete them using information from the text.

Answers

1. The poet sets up the tent in a <u>field</u>. [1 mark]
2. At <u>night</u>, she can hear an owl. [1 mark]
3. She can also hear the <u>rain</u> dripping onto it. [1 mark]
4. She loves it best when the sun shines. [1 mark]
5. The sun makes the tent <u>glow</u> like gold. [1 mark]

Try these

Assist children if they ask for help with vocabulary, first discussing what they think the words might mean. Ask children to write sentences to answer

Unit 2: Poetry: 'I Love Our Orange Tent'

the questions, explaining their answers with reference to the text and their own experiences.

Suggested answers

1. *When she is in the tent, the poet can hear an owl crying, the tent flapping and the rain pattering.* *[example]*
2. The poet also uses the senses of smell and sight to describe her experiences with the tent. [1 mark]
3. A simile is a description that compares one thing with another. [1 mark]
4. The three other similes in the poem are 'like a flying bird', 'like yellow honey' and 'like gold'. [3 marks]
5. No, the poet does not go camping on her own. I think this because the poem says, 'When we're lying in it', which suggests she is with at least one other person. She also says 'We plant it'. [1 mark]

Now try these

Open-ended questions

1. Answers should recognise that the line's repetition emphasises its importance, and helps the reader to understand how much the poet loves the tent. [1 mark]
2. Diary entries should be from the poet's point of view and refer to the kinds of experiences that are included in the poem, without repeating them. [3 mark max]
3. Answers should contain four reasonable ideas for similes describing an interest or hobby. [1 mark per simile]

Support, embed & challenge

Support

Use Unit 2 Resource 1: Similes to support children if they still struggle to understand the concept of a simile. Remind children of the line in the poem, 'We plant it like a flower in the field', and point out that the tent is compared to a flower. Explain that we call a comparison like this a simile. Show the children the worksheet and read the first part of each simile aloud. Ask them to find and match the parts of the four similes in the poem. Then read some of the possible ways to complete the other similes, and talk about which might constitute a suitable ending. Ask children, possibly in pairs, to draw lines to complete the similes appropriately. (**Answers** We plant it like a flower in a field; My tent flaps like a flying bird; It pours in like yellow honey; It glows like gold; The snow glitters like diamonds; She dances like a ballerina; He ran home like a galloping horse; They fought like cats and dogs; Your cheeks are red like roses; I slept like a log)

Embed

Use Unit 2 Resource 2: My descriptive poem to encourage children to apply their learning by planning their own poems to describe an interesting experience. Ask them to complete the planning grid by thinking about the sights, smells, noises, tastes and feelings of the experience. Encourage them to include some similes, too.

Challenge

Challenge children to find further examples of similes in poetry and then to create some of their own. They should then use them in a descriptive poem.

Homework / Additional activities

The new tent

Ask children to imagine they are the speaker in the poem. Then ask them to imagine that, when they are about to prepare for a camping trip, their parents have discovered that the orange tent has torn! Their parents buy a new tent: a big, green one. Ask children to write a diary extract about their feelings.

Collins Connect: Unit 2

Ask the children to complete Unit 2 (see Teach → Year 4 → Comprehension → Unit 2).

Unit 3: Poetry: 'The Donkey'

Overview

English curriculum objectives

- Listen to and discuss a wide range of fiction, poetry, plays, non-fiction and reference books or textbooks
- Read books that are structured in different ways and reading for a range of purposes
- Use dictionaries to check the meanings of words they have read
- Identify themes and conventions in a wide range of books
- Prepare poems and playscripts to read aloud and to perform, showing understanding through intonation, tone, volume and action
- Discuss words and phrases that capture the reader's interest and imagination
- Recognise some different forms of poetry
- Check that the text makes sense to them, discussing their understanding and explaining the meaning of words in context
- Ask questions to improve their understanding of a text
- Draw inferences such as inferring characters' feelings, thoughts and motives from their actions, and justifying inferences with evidence
- Identify how language, structure and presentation contribute to meaning
- Participate in discussion about both books that are read to them and those they can read for themselves, taking turns and listening to what others say

Treasure House resources

- Comprehension Skills Pupil Book 4, Unit 3, pages 10–12
- Collins Connect Treasure House Comprehension Year 4, Unit 3
- Photocopiable Unit 3, Resource 1: Comparing animals, page 69
- Photocopiable Unit 3, Resource 2: My new-born animal poem, page 70

Additional resources

- Dictionaries or the internet (optional)
- Other poems about new-born or vulnerable animals (optional)

Introduction

Teaching overview

'The Donkey' is a descriptive poem about a new-born familiar creature. It describes how delicate and fragile a one-day-old donkey appears. The poem contains examples of similes and a simple rhyming pattern, where alternate lines rhyme (ABCBDEFE).

Introduce the poem

Ask the children to tell you everything they can imagine about a new-born donkey. On the board write 'The Donkey', and create a mind map as the children contribute their ideas. Ask: 'What do new-born donkeys look like?', 'How do they behave?', 'What do they eat?', 'Where do they live?'

Tell the children that, in this lesson, they will focus on a poem about a new-born donkey. Then they will answer questions about it. Remind children that sometimes the answers to the questions will be clearly written in the poem, but that sometimes they may need to think a little harder and use their own ideas, supported by the text.

Ask the children to read the poem individually or in pairs. Ask them to note down any words they do not understand. Discuss unknown or unusual vocabulary before setting children to work answering the questions in the Pupil Book. Try to avoid discussing the content of the poem until after the children have answered the questions.

Pupil practice

Pupil Book pages 10–12

Get started

Children copy the sentences and complete them using information from the text.

Answers

1. The donkey was <u>one day</u> old. [1 mark]
2. His <u>neck</u> seemed too small for his <u>head</u>. [1 mark]
3. He had a soft, grey <u>coat</u>. [1 mark]
4. The poet thought the donkey's face looked <u>wistful</u>. [1 mark]
5. Eventually, the donkey lay down to <u>rest</u> on the ground. [1 mark]

26

Unit 3: Poetry: 'The Donkey'

Try these
Assist children if they ask for help with vocabulary, first discussing what they think the words might mean. Ask children to write sentences to answer the questions, explaining their answers with reference to the text and their own experiences.

Suggested answers
1. *The donkey couldn't move around well because it was very young and just learning to walk. [example]*
2. The words 'gambol' and 'frisk' mean run, skip or leap playfully, 'blundered' means made mistakes or was clumsy, 'venturesome' means adventurous and 'quest' means journey or search. [5 marks]
3. These words make me think that the donkey is trying to learn to have fun and discover new things, but it isn't able to do it properly yet. [1 mark]
4. I think the poet liked / was fascinated by / was worried for the donkey. I think this because he called the donkey 'lovely' / watched him for a long time / prayed for him. [1 mark]
5. I think the poet prayed for the donkey because he looked so fragile. [1 mark]

Now try these
Open-ended questions
1. Questions and ideas should be from the donkey's point of view, and refer to the problems and situation he faces in the poem. Ideas should be about what he might try to do next. [3 marks max]
2. Rhyming words: 'old'/'hold'; 'loose'/'use'; 'bit'/'it'; 'grey'/'way'; 'doubt'/'about'; 'quest'/'rest'; 'slim'/'him'. [1 mark]
   Open-ended question: Children should write eight new lines about the donkey. The end words of lines 2 and 4, and lines 6 and 8, should rhyme. [4 marks max]
3. Pictures should be relevant to the extract, including details it mentions. [3 marks max]

Support, embed & challenge

Support
Use Unit 3 Resource 1: Comparing animals to support children in extracting information from the poem and thinking about the qualities of the new-born donkey that it describes. Ask children to fill in information about the donkey from the poem and their own experiences. Discuss why the author may have chosen to include the information that they did in the poem. Then ask children to choose two further animals and complete the table.

Embed
Use Unit 3 Resource 2: My new-born animal poem to encourage children to create their own poems using a style similar to that of 'The Donkey'. Re-read the poem then read the structure and support provided on the worksheet. Ask children to choose an animal then to begin to create their poems.

Challenge
Challenge children to research and write a list of the correct names for baby animals. They can be unusual! For example, a baby alpaca is called a 'cria'. You could add a competitive element by challenging the children to see which pair can find most words – or the most unusual ones!

Homework / Additional activities

A thoughtful verse
Ask children to write a short, original poem inspired by these lines:

'His face was wistful
And left no doubt
That he felt life needed
Some thinking about.'

The poem doesn't need to rhyme.

Collins Connect: Unit 3
Ask the children to complete Unit 3 (see Teach → Year 4 → Comprehension → Unit 3).

Unit 4: Non-fiction (newspaper report): The Accident

Overview

English curriculum objectives

- Listen to and discuss a wide range of fiction, poetry, plays, non-fiction and reference books or textbooks
- Read books that are structured in different ways and reading for a range of purposes
- Use dictionaries to check the meanings of words they have read
- Identify themes and conventions in a wide range of books
- Discuss words and phrases that capture the reader's interest and imagination
- Check that the text makes sense to them, discussing their understanding and explaining the meaning of words in context
- Ask questions to improve their understanding of a text
- Draw inferences such as inferring characters' feelings, thoughts and motives from their actions, and justifying inferences with evidence
- Predict what might happen from details stated and implied
- Identify main ideas drawn from more than one paragraph and summarise these
- Identify how language, structure and presentation contribute to meaning
- Retrieve and record information from non-fiction
- Participate in discussion about both books that are read to them and those they can read for themselves, taking turns and listening to what others say

Treasure House resources

- Comprehension Skills Pupil Book 4, Unit 4, pages 13–15
- Collins Connect Treasure House Comprehension Year 4, Unit 4
- Photocopiable Unit 4, Resource 1: Find the facts, page 71
- Photocopiable Unit 4, Resource 2: Tell the story, page 72

Additional resources

- Dictionaries or the internet (optional)
- Examples of real local news reports (optional)

Introduction

Teaching overview

'The Accident' is a fictional news report about an elderly lady who fell through the ice on a frozen river while walking her sister's dog. The report provides a simple example of a formal, impersonal news report with characteristics such as eye witness quotes and facts detailing what happened, when, where, why and to whom.

Introduce the text

Ask the children if they ever read reports in newspapers. If they do, invite them to share their experiences with the class. Ask: 'Why do you think people read newspapers?' Clarify that newspapers provide us with both entertaining reports and serious news information about things that happen locally, nationally and internationally.

Tell the children that, in this lesson, they will focus on a serious (but fictional) newspaper report about an elderly lady who has an accident. Then they will answer questions about it. Remind children that sometimes the answers to the questions will be clearly written in the report, but that sometimes they may need to think a little harder and use their own ideas, supported by the text.

Ask the children to read the report individually or in pairs. Ask them to note down any words they do not understand. Discuss unknown or unusual vocabulary before setting children to work answering the questions in the Pupil Book. Try to avoid discussing the content of the report until after the children have answered the questions.

Unit 4: Non-fiction (newspaper report): The Accident

Pupil practice

Pupil Book pages 13–15

Get started

Children copy the sentences and complete them using information from the text.

Answers

1. Yesterday, an elderly lady fell through the <u>ice</u>. [1 mark]
2. The River <u>Thames</u> had frozen over. [1 mark]
3. Mrs Wills lived in <u>Onslow</u> <u>Gardens</u>. [1 mark]
4. Mrs Wills was <u>79</u> years old. [1 mark]
5. The dog was a black <u>Labrador</u>. [1 mark]

Try these

Assist children if they ask for help with vocabulary, first discussing what they think the words might mean. Ask children to write sentences to answer the questions, explaining their answers with reference to the text and their own experiences.

Suggested answers

1. *Never, as this was the first time in living memory that the River Thames had frozen from bank to bank.* [example]
2. No one: Mrs Wills had been walking alone with the dog. [1 mark]
3. Mrs Wills didn't survive because the water was so cold. [1 mark]
4. I think Mrs Wills went onto the ice to try to fetch her sister's dog, not expecting it to break. [1 mark]
5. I do not think it would be safe to play on the frozen Thames. I think this because Mrs Wills and an eight-year-old boy both fell through the ice. [1 mark]

Now try these

Open-ended questions

1. Sentences should be from the point of view of someone who saw the accident, reacting appropriately. [3 marks max]
2. Look for dramatic language and clear descriptions to match the style of the news report. The paragraphs may or may not include the interview with the bystander or information on what happened to the dog, but should contribute new information. [3 marks max]
3. Posters should be well presented and give information clearly. They should warn people of the risk of falling through the ice and the freezing temperature of the water. [3 marks max]

Support, embed & challenge

Support

Use Unit 4 Resource 1: Find the facts to support children in extracting the facts from the newspaper report. Read through the table and discuss where each piece of information is in the report. Discuss the difference between 'why' and 'how': 'why' asks for reasons and motivations, whereas 'how' asks for a description of the manner in which an event occurred.

Embed

Use Unit 4 Resource 2: Tell the story to encourage children to apply their understanding of the events described by rewriting them as a narrative story. Remind them that narratives can have more description and dialogue than a newspaper report usually does.

Challenge

Challenge children to write a newspaper report about an event that has recently happened at school. Ask different pairs of children to write about different events or school-related topics, and then collate all of the articles to make a class newspaper.

Homework / Additional activities

Real-life reports

Ask children to find an interesting news report at home to bring in and show to the class. Ask them to isolate the facts detailing what happened, when, where, why and to whom, and to notice other features such as interviews with people involved.

Collins Connect: Unit 4

Ask the children to complete Unit 4 (see Teach → Year 4 → Comprehension → Unit 4).

Unit 5: Non-fiction (diary): Holiday diary

Overview

English curriculum objectives

- Listen to and discuss a wide range of fiction, poetry, plays, non-fiction and reference books or textbooks
- Read books that are structured in different ways and reading for a range of purposes
- Use dictionaries to check the meanings of words they have read
- Identify themes and conventions in a wide range of books
- Discuss words and phrases that capture the reader's interest and imagination
- Check that the text makes sense to them, discussing their understanding and explaining the meaning of words in context
- Ask questions to improve their understanding of a text
- Draw inferences such as inferring characters' feelings, thoughts and motives from their actions, and justifying inferences with evidence
- Predict what might happen from details stated and implied
- Identify main ideas drawn from more than one paragraph and summarise these
- Identify how language, structure and presentation contribute to meaning
- Retrieve and record information from non-fiction
- Participate in discussion about both books that are read to them and those they can read for themselves, taking turns and listening to what others say

Treasure House resources

- Comprehension Skills Pupil Book 4, Unit 5, pages 16–18
- Collins Connect Treasure House Comprehension Year 4, Unit 5
- Photocopiable Unit 5, Resource 1: A letter from the pilot, page 73
- Photocopiable Unit 5, Resource 2: A news report, page 74

Additional resources

- Dictionaries or the internet (optional)
- Other examples of first-person narration (optional)

Introduction

Teaching overview

'Holiday diary' is an extract from the (fictional) diary of a girl called Meena. Meena is on holiday with her family, and her diary describes her feelings and actions, and the exciting events with which she becomes involved when she and a new friend save the life of a pilot. It features characteristics typical of diaries: date headings, further subheadings (such as 'Later …'), chronological order and first-person narration.

Introduce the text

Ask the children if any of them writes a diary. If they do, invite them to share their reasons and experiences with the class. Then discuss further why someone might want to keep a diary. Take suggestions, and establish that some people like to write a diary to help them express their feelings and/or to remember events.

Tell the children that, in this lesson, they will focus on a series of diary entries that tell the reader about a girl called Meena and her experiences on holiday. Then they will answer questions about it. Remind children that sometimes the answers to the questions will be clearly written in the entries, but that sometimes they may need to think a little harder and use their own ideas, supported by the text.

Ask the children to read the diary entries individually or in pairs. Ask them to note down any words they do not understand. Discuss unknown or unusual vocabulary before setting children to work answering the questions in the Pupil Book. Try to avoid discussing the content of the entries until after the children have answered the questions.

Unit 5: Non-fiction (diary): Holiday diary

Pupil practice

Pupil Book pages 16–18

Get started
Children copy the sentences and complete them using information from the text.

Answers
1. The girl writing the diary is called <u>Meena</u>. [1 mark]
2. Her mum and dad felt <u>exhausted</u> on Friday. [1 mark]
3. Raj didn't want to do <u>anything</u> interesting. [1 mark]
4. The two girls met on <u>Friday</u> afternoon. [1 mark]
5. Stacey went to Meena's holiday house on <u>Saturday</u>. [1 mark]

Try these
Assist children if they ask for help with vocabulary, first discussing what they think the words might mean. Ask children to write sentences to answer the questions, explaining their answers with reference to the text and their own experiences.

Suggested answers
1. *The girls knew the pilot ejected because they could see him floating down by parachute.* [example]
2. Air-Sea Rescue arrived to help the pilot, in an orange helicopter. [1 mark]
3. I think Raj is Meena's brother. I think this because he is on holiday with her and her parents, and she wants him to play with her. [1 mark]
4. When she gets over her shock, I think Meena will feel proud and glad about what happened on Saturday and still hope that the pilot is OK. [1 mark]
5. I think Meena's mum feels proud. I think this because she says Stacey and Meena probably saved the pilot's life. [1 mark]

Now try these
Open-ended questions
1. Sentences should be from Stacey's point of view, reacting to what she and Meena did to save the pilot. [3 marks max]
2. Diary entries should be consistent with the extract, including the characters of Meena, Stacey, Raj and Meena's parents, and include diary features like the date and chatty, first-person narration. [3 marks max]
3. Pictures should be relevant to the extract, and could feature labels and/or notes clarifying what happened. [3 marks max]

Support, embed & challenge

Support
Use Unit 5 Resource 1: A letter from the pilot to support children in their understanding of the events in the diary entries, and their impacts, by writing a thank-you letter to Meena and Stacey from the pilot using the sentence starters on the template.

Embed
Use Unit 5 Resource 2: A news report to encourage children to apply their understanding of the events in the diary entries by writing a newspaper report about them. Remind them to give details that describe what happened, when, where, why and to whom. Support children to make plans if necessary.

Challenge
Challenge children to write their own diary entries about something else that happens to Meena and Stacey, or to new characters of their choice. Remind them to use diary features such as dates and chatty, first-person narration.

Homework / Additional activities

My diary
Ask children to write their own series of diary entries over a weekend, week or a holiday period. Ask them to be prepared to share their diaries (so they can choose not to write anything too personal).

Collins Connect: Unit 5
Ask the children to complete Unit 5 (see Teach → Year 4 → Comprehension → Unit 5).

Unit 6: Fiction (fable): 'The Eagle and the Turtle'

Overview

English curriculum objectives

- Listen to and discuss a wide range of fiction, poetry, plays, non-fiction and reference books or textbooks
- Read books that are structured in different ways and reading for a range of purposes
- Use dictionaries to check the meanings of words they have read
- Increase their familiarity with a wide range of books, including fairy stories, myths and legends, and retell some of these orally
- Identify themes and conventions in a wide range of books
- Discuss words and phrases that capture the reader's interest and imagination
- Check that the text makes sense to them, discussing their understanding and explaining the meaning of words in context
- Ask questions to improve their understanding of a text
- Draw inferences such as inferring characters' feelings, thoughts and motives from their actions, and justifying inferences with evidence
- Predict what might happen from details stated and implied
- Identify main ideas drawn from more than one paragraph and summarise these
- Identify how language, structure and presentation contribute to meaning
- Participate in discussion about both books that are read to them and those they can read for themselves, taking turns and listening to what others say

Treasure House resources

- Comprehension Skills Pupil Book 4, Unit 6, pages 19–21
- Collins Connect Treasure House Comprehension Year 4, Unit 6
- Photocopiable Unit 6, Resource 1: Making decisions, page 75
- Photocopiable Unit 6, Resource 2: A story of advice, page 76

Additional resources

- Dictionaries or the internet (optional)
- Other fables by Aesop (optional)

Introduction

Teaching overview

'The Eagle and the Turtle' is a version of the traditional fable by Aesop. It tells the tale of a turtle that is not satisfied with his life. He decides he wants to fly, and persuades an eagle to carry him up to the sky. Of course, when the eagle lets go, the turtle falls to the ground. The moral of the tale is to 'be satisfied with what you are'.

Introduce the story

Ask the children if any of them know the fable of the Eagle and the Turtle, or any other fables. If they do, invite them to share their knowledge and experience of fables' structures with the class.

Tell the children that, in this lesson, they will focus on one version of the story, which was originally attributed to a storyteller called Aesop over 2500 years ago. Then they will answer questions about it. Remind children that sometimes the answers to the questions will be clearly written in the story, but that sometimes they may need to think a little harder and use their own ideas, supported by the text.

Ask the children to read the story individually or in pairs. Ask them to note down any words they do not understand. Discuss unknown or unusual vocabulary before setting children to work answering the questions in the Pupil Book. Try to avoid discussing the content of the story until after the children have answered the questions.

Pupil practice

Pupil Book pages 19–21

Get started

Children copy the sentences and complete them using information from the text.

Answers

1. The Turtle was not <u>satisfied</u> with being a turtle. [1 mark]
2. He was <u>tired</u> of swimming about in the sea. [1 mark]
3. He decided to speak to the <u>Eagle</u> about his problem. [1 mark]
4. The Eagle told the Turtle he wasn't <u>built</u> for flying. [1 mark]

32

Unit 6: Fiction (fable): 'The Eagle and the Turtle'

5. But the Turtle insisted the Eagle carry him as high as the <u>clouds</u>. [1 mark]

Try these
Assist children if they ask for help with vocabulary, first discussing what they think the words might mean. Ask children to write sentences to answer the questions, explaining their answers with reference to the text and their own experiences.

Suggested answers

1. *The Turtle was unhappy with his life because he was tired of getting nowhere in particular.* [example]
2. The Turtle thought his four flippers would be as good as wings. [1 mark]
3. You should learn to accept there are things you can't do. / You should be happy with the skills you have. (Answers should paraphrase, not repeat, the moral given: 'Be satisfied with what you are.') [1 mark]
4. I think the Eagle agreed to carry the Turtle into the clouds because he wanted the pearls from the sea. / I think the Eagle agreed to carry the Turtle into the clouds because he wanted to see what would happen. / I think the Eagle agreed to carry the Turtle into the clouds because he wanted to prove the Turtle wrong. [1 mark]
5. I think the Eagle expected the Turtle to fall because he said the Turtle was not built for flying. / I think the Eagle hoped the Turtle would fly, so he could give him the pearls. [1 mark]

Now try these
Open-ended questions

1. Sentences should be from the Eagle's point of view, and say what he really thinks of the Turtle. (For example: I think the Turtle is silly and deserves to be proved wrong. / I think the Turtle might be right – I'll help him.) [3 marks max]
2. Retellings should attempt to consider the Eagle's perspective, intentions and opinions, and still contain the major events of the original tale. [3 marks max]
3. Pictures should be relevant to the extract, including details it mentions. Thought bubbles should contain thoughts from each character's perspective that are relevant to the context. [3 marks max]

Support, embed & challenge

Support
Use Unit 6 Resource 1: Making decisions to support children in thinking about the decisions made by the Turtle and the Eagle, and how things might have worked out differently if they had made different decisions. Support the children to complete the tables through discussion, where necessary.

Embed
Use Unit 6 Resource 2: A story of advice to encourage children to apply their learning to develop their own stories based on advice. They may or may not choose to use one of the example pieces of advice given, 'be careful what you wish for' or 'you don't know what you've got until it's gone'.

Challenge
Challenge children to think about how other children could be encouraged to be satisfied with whom they are and what they have. Ask groups to plan, and then individuals to begin writing, a story to persuade others of the meaning and importance of contentment.

Homework / Additional activities

Creature discomforts
Ask children to write a list of animals and, next to each animal, to note down what may cause that animal to feel dissatisfied. For example, a fish could feel dissatisfied that it is unable to walk on land. You could choose to add a competitive element by challenging the children to see who can write the longest list.

(This activity could also be expanded into a creative writing exercise that uses one point of dissatisfaction as the basis for a story similar to 'The Eagle and the Turtle'.)

Collins Connect: Unit 6
Ask the children to complete Unit 6 (see Teach → Year 4 → Comprehension → Unit 6).

Unit 7: Fiction (classic): 'Cockadoodle-Doo, Mr Sultana!'

Overview

English curriculum objectives

- Listen to and discuss a wide range of fiction, poetry, plays, non-fiction and reference books or textbooks
- Read books that are structured in different ways and reading for a range of purposes
- Use dictionaries to check the meanings of words they have read
- Increase their familiarity with a wide range of books, including fairy stories, myths and legends, and retell some of these orally
- Identify themes and conventions in a wide range of books
- Discuss words and phrases that capture the reader's interest and imagination
- Check that the text makes sense to them, discussing their understanding and explaining the meaning of words in context
- Ask questions to improve their understanding of a text
- Draw inferences such as inferring characters' feelings, thoughts and motives from their actions, and justifying inferences with evidence
- Predict what might happen from details stated and implied
- Identify main ideas drawn from more than one paragraph and summarise these
- Identify how language, structure and presentation contribute to meaning
- Participate in discussion about both books that are read to them and those they can read for themselves, taking turns and listening to what others say

Treasure House resources

- Comprehension Skills Pupil Book 4, Unit 7, pages 22–24
- Collins Connect Treasure House Comprehension Year 4, Unit 7
- Photocopiable Unit 7, Resource 1: Before and after, page 77
- Photocopiable Unit 7, Resource 2: Finders keepers!, page 78

Additional resources

- Dictionaries or the internet (optional)
- *Cockadoodle-Doo, Mr Sultana!* by Michael Morpurgo, whole text (optional)

Introduction

Teaching overview

Cockadoodle-Doo, Mr Sultana! is the story of a little red rooster who discovers something unexpectedly valuable while pecking around in the dirt one day. He has to choose between loyalty to his sovereign and to his mistress – but, in the trouble caused by this choice, he literally loses sight of what caused his dilemma.

Introduce the extract

Ask the children if any of them know the story *Cockadoodle-Doo, Mr Sultana!* If they do, invite them to share their knowledge with the class. Then ask if anyone remembers having or seeing an argument that got so overblown that the main point was forgotten. Again, ask them to share any experiences with the class.

Tell the children that, in this lesson, they will focus on one extract from a story about a quarrel between a little rooster and a sultan. Then they will answer questions about it. Remind children that sometimes the answers to the questions will be clearly written in the extract, but that sometimes they may need to think a little harder and use their own ideas, supported by the text.

Ask the children to read the extract individually or in pairs. Ask them to note down any words they do not understand. Discuss unknown or unusual vocabulary before setting children to work answering the questions in the Pupil Book. Try to avoid discussing the content of the extract until after the children have answered the questions.

34

Unit 7: Fiction (classic): 'Cockadoodle-Doo, Mr Sultana!'

Pupil practice

Pupil Book pages 22–24

Get started
Children copy the sentences and complete them using information from the text.

Answers
1. The main character of this story is the little red rooster. [1 mark]
2. He found something shiny on the dusty farm track by the cornfield. [1 mark]
3. The shiny item was a diamond button. [1 mark]
4. The button belonged to the Sultan. [1 mark]
5. The rooster ran away into the cornfield, but he dropped the button! [1 mark]

Try these
Assist children if they ask for help with vocabulary, first discussing what they think the words might mean. Ask children to write sentences to answer the questions, explaining their answers with reference to the text and their own experiences.

Suggested answers
1. *The Sultan wanted the button back because it was very valuable. [example]*
2. A 'sultan' is a ruler or king. A 'sultana' is a raisin without seeds (or the female partner of a sultan). I think a 'kerfuffle' is a scuffle or fuss. [1 mark]
3. The little red rooster wanted to give the item to his mistress because she loves pretty things / because she has nothing pretty of her own / so she wouldn't be cross with him for running away / because she needs the button a lot more than the Sultan does. (Three of these reasons should be given.) [3 marks max]
4. I think the little red rooster felt brave / confident / annoyed / loyal to his mistress when he was asked to give the button back. (The one answer that children should not give is that the rooster felt frightened.) [1 mark]
5. I do not think the Sultan expected this response as he was used to being obeyed by his servants and subjects. [1 mark]

Now try these
Open-ended questions
1. Sentences should be from the Sultan's point of view, reacting to the rooster arguing with him and refusing to give him back the diamond button. [3 marks max]
2. New endings should be relevant to the events of the extract, especially regarding the mistress's character and circumstances, and the anger of the Sultan. [3 marks max]
3. Pictures should be relevant to the extract, including details it mentions. Thought bubbles should contain thoughts from each character's perspective that are relevant to the context. [3 marks max]

Support, embed & challenge

Support
Use Unit 7 Resource 1: Before and after to support children in thinking about how finding the diamond button affected the little red rooster. Encourage children to use the extract and their imagination to complete the table.

Embed
Use Unit 7 Resource 2: Finders keepers! to encourage children to plan their own short stories about a disagreement over a found object.

Ask: 'Should the original owner get the item back, or is it a case of 'finders keepers'?'

Challenge
Challenge children to think about what they would have done if they had been the little red rooster and had found the diamond button. Ask the children to write a list of reasons the button should be returned to the Sultan, and a list of reasons it should be given to the rooster's mistress. Ask the children to discuss the problem in groups, and reach a conclusion about what they would do.

Homework / Additional activities

What happens next?
Ask children to think about what could happen next in the story. Ask: 'Which story will we follow: the story of the rooster, the story of the Sultan or the story of the diamond button itself?' Ask children to choose one track, and to show their ideas through writing and/or pictures.

Collins Connect: Unit 7
Ask the children to complete Unit 7 (see Teach → Year 4 → Comprehension → Unit 7).

Review unit 1: Fiction: 'Aladdin and the Genies' Pupil Book pages 25–27

Get started
Children copy the sentences and complete them using information from the text.

Answers

1. The notice was <u>pinned</u> on the town gate. [1 mark]
2. "We don't <u>know anything</u> about this Kadar Ghazi." [1 mark]
3. Trying not to feel too hopeful, Aladdin soon found the <u>blue door</u>. [1 mark]
4. Wondering what would happen next, he <u>decided</u> to wait for a while. [1 mark]
5. A door in the wall swung open, and an <u>enormous</u> man dressed in shimmering silk appeared. [1 mark]

Try these
Assist children if they ask for help with vocabulary, first discussing what they think the words might mean. Ask children to write sentences to answer the questions, explaining their answers with reference to the text or their own experiences.

Suggested answers

1. *Kadar Ghazi the merchant placed the notice.* [example]
2. The notice was designed to find a clever young boy who wants to be rich and is willing to obey orders without asking questions. [2 marks]
3. Aladdin is suitable for the job as he is a clever young boy who wants to be rich. He is unsuitable as he is always asking questions. [2 marks]
4. I think Aladdin's mother wants him to be careful as they don't know anything about Kadar Ghazi / as she finds the notice suspicious / as she thinks Aladdin will ask questions and get into trouble. [2 marks max]
5. I think the purpose of the dark and empty room was to test whether or not people responding to the notice would be too scared to wait. [1 mark]

Now try these
Open-ended questions

1. Sentences should be from Kadar Ghazi's point of view, giving his first impressions of Aladdin (who has been awaiting him without fear in the dark room). [3 marks max]
2. Retellings should be from Aladdin's mother's point of view, and include all the plot details given in Chapter 1. [3 marks max]
3. Pictures should be relevant to the extract, including details it mentions. Speech should consider the points of view of Aladdin and Kadar Ghazi after they meet. [3 marks max]

Unit 8: Fiction (classic): 'The Wind in the Willows'

Overview

English curriculum objectives

- Listen to and discuss a wide range of fiction, poetry, plays, non-fiction and reference books or textbooks
- Read books that are structured in different ways and reading for a range of purposes
- Use dictionaries to check the meanings of words they have read
- Increase their familiarity with a wide range of books, including fairy stories, myths and legends, and retell some of these orally
- Identify themes and conventions in a wide range of books
- Discuss words and phrases that capture the reader's interest and imagination
- Check that the text makes sense to them, discussing their understanding and explaining the meaning of words in context
- Ask questions to improve their understanding of a text
- Draw inferences such as inferring characters' feelings, thoughts and motives from their actions, and justifying inferences with evidence
- Predict what might happen from details stated and implied
- Identify main ideas drawn from more than one paragraph and summarise these
- Identify how language, structure and presentation contribute to meaning
- Participate in discussion about both books that are read to them and those they can read for themselves, taking turns and listening to what others say

Treasure House resources

- Comprehension Skills Pupil Book 4, Unit 8, pages 28–30
- Collins Connect Treasure House Comprehension Year 4, Unit 8
- Photocopiable Unit 8, Resource 1: Asking questions, page 79
- Photocopiable Unit 8, Resource 2: The next adventure, page 80

Additional resources

- Dictionaries or the internet (optional)
- *The Wind in the Willows* by Kenneth Grahame, whole text (optional)

Introduction

Teaching overview

The Wind in the Willows is a classic children's novel by Kenneth Grahame, first published in 1908. In the extract, Mole takes a break from spring-cleaning his underground home and ends up at the river, which he has never seen before. Here he meets Rat, who spends his days on or near the river, with his little blue rowing boat. Rat and Mole go for a ride in Rat's boat and begin a deep and lasting friendship.

Introduce the extract

Ask the children if any of them has ever read or heard the story of *The Wind in the Willows*. If they have, invite them to share their experiences with the class.

Tell the children that, in this lesson, they will focus on one extract from the story in which two main characters first get acquainted. Then they will answer questions about it. Remind children that sometimes the answers to the questions will be clearly written in the extract, but that sometimes they may need to think a little harder and use their own ideas, supported by the text.

Ask the children to read the extract individually or in pairs. Ask them to note down any words they do not understand. Discuss unknown or unusual vocabulary before setting children to work answering the questions in the Pupil Book. Try to avoid discussing the content of the extract until after the children have answered the questions.

Unit 8: Fiction (classic): 'The Wind in the Willows'

Pupil practice

Pupil Book pages 28–30

Get started
Children copy the sentences and complete them using information from the text.

Answers
1. The Mole had needed a rest from <u>spring-cleaning</u> his house. [1 mark]
2. He was sitting on the grass next to the <u>river</u>. [1 mark]
3. The Water Rat had silky hair and small neat <u>ears</u>. [1 mark]
4. The boat was just the size for <u>two animals</u>. [1 mark]
5. The Mole had <u>never</u> been in a boat before. [1 mark]

Try these
Assist children if they ask for help with vocabulary, first discussing what they think the words might mean. Ask children to write sentences to answer the questions, explaining their answers with reference to the text and their own experiences.

Suggested answers
1. *The Mole couldn't see the Water Rat's eye properly at first because the Water Rat was in a dark hole.* [example]
2. The word 'stooped' means bent down, 'hauled' means pulled, 'sculled' means rowed and 'rapture' means intense happiness. [4 marks]
3. The mole was intensely happy to be in the boat. [1 mark]
4. The Mole did not expect the Water Rat to invite him onto the boat. I know this because he felt 'surprise' when he was 'actually' sitting in a 'real boat'. [2 marks max]
5. I do not think the Mole and the Water Rat already knew each other because the Mole didn't recognise the Water Rat and hadn't been in his boat before. / I think the Mole and the Water Rat did already know each other because the Water Rat came over to see the Mole at once. [2 marks]

Now try these
Open-ended questions
1. Sentences should be from the Water Rat's point of view, reacting to seeing and then meeting the Mole. They could describe seeing the Mole in a similar way to that in which the extract describes the Mole seeing the Water Rat. [3 marks max]
2. Retellings should attempt to consider the Water Rat's perspective, intentions and feelings. [3 marks max]
3. Pictures should be relevant to the extract, including details it mentions. They should include the Water Rat rowing his blue boat towards the Mole. [3 marks max]

Support, embed & challenge

Support
Use Unit 8 Resource 1: Asking questions to support children in considering the nature of the Rat and the Mole's friendship. Once they have reread the extract, ask them what questions the Mole and the Rat could ask to get to know each other better. Talk about the importance of being interested in other people's lives and asking questions as a way of building a friendship. Ask children to list as many questions as they can.

Embed
Use Unit 8 Resource 2: The next adventure to encourage children to use their understanding of the characters and settings by planning to write the next part of the story, in which the Mole and the Rat have an adventure in the boat. Ask: 'Will the Mole like the boat?', 'What might the animals see?'

Challenge
Challenge children to research and create a glossary of boating terms.

Homework / Additional activities

Others in the willows
If possible, ask children to read more of *The Wind in the Willows*. Ask them to list other characters that are in the story later on and to describe them briefly, using the Mole's description of Rat ('Small neat ears and thick silky hair') as a template.

Collins Connect: Unit 8
Ask the children to complete Unit 8 (see Teach → Year 4 → Comprehension → Unit 8).

Unit 9: Fiction (historical): 'Stowaway!'

Overview

English curriculum objectives

- Listen to and discuss a wide range of fiction, poetry, plays, non-fiction and reference books or textbooks
- Read books that are structured in different ways and reading for a range of purposes
- Use dictionaries to check the meanings of words they have read
- Increase their familiarity with a wide range of books, including fairy stories, myths and legends, and retell some of these orally
- Identify themes and conventions in a wide range of books
- Discuss words and phrases that capture the reader's interest and imagination
- Check that the text makes sense to them, discussing their understanding and explaining the meaning of words in context
- Ask questions to improve their understanding of a text
- Draw inferences such as inferring characters' feelings, thoughts and motives from their actions, and justifying inferences with evidence
- Predict what might happen from details stated and implied
- Identify main ideas drawn from more than one paragraph and summarise these
- Identify how language, structure and presentation contribute to meaning
- Participate in discussion about both books that are read to them and those they can read for themselves, taking turns and listening to what others say

Treasure House resources

- Comprehension Skills Pupil Book 4, Unit 9, pages 31–33
- Collins Connect Treasure House Comprehension Year 4, Unit 9
- Photocopiable Unit 9, Resource 1: Dickon's character, page 81
- Photocopiable Unit 9, Resource 2: A story starts, page 82

Additional resources

- Dictionaries or the internet (optional)
- *Stowaway!* by Julia Jarman, whole text (optional)

Introduction

Teaching overview

Stowaway! by Julia Jarman is a historical adventure that tells the story of a young Tudor boy called Dickon in the 16th century, and his dream to sail with the famous Captain Francis Drake. Turned away from being a cabin boy because of his lame leg, Dickon is asked to carry a bag aboard the 'Pelican' by Drake's cousin. He then stows away on the ship. During the twists and turns of the adventure that follows the extract, readers gain an insight into the harsh life experienced by sailors in Tudor times, witnessing storms, mutiny and sickness on board.

Introduce the extract

Ask the children if any of them knows the story *Stowaway!* If they do, invite them to share their knowledge with the class. Then ask children if they know anything about early sailing or explorers, and again ask them to share their knowledge. Give some basic historical background about Sir Francis Drake: He was an English sea captain in the late 1500s. He carried out the second-ever trip all around the world in a single expedition, on a ship called the 'Pelican', from 1577 to 1580. He is considered a great hero in England, but often a ruthless pirate in other countries!

Tell the children that, in this lesson, they will focus on one extract from the story. Then they will answer questions about it. Remind children that sometimes the answers to the questions will be clearly written in the extract, but that sometimes they may need to think a little harder and use their own ideas, supported by the text.

Ask the children to read the extract individually or in pairs. Ask them to note down any words they do not understand. Discuss unknown or unusual vocabulary before setting children to work answering the questions in the Pupil Book. Try to avoid discussing the content of the extract until after the children have answered the questions.

Unit 9: Fiction (historical): 'Stowaway!'

Pupil practice

Pupil Book pages 31–33

Get started
Children copy the sentences and complete them using information from the text.

Answers
1. Dickon/Tib and Tib/Dickon were best friends. [1 mark]
2. Francis Drake was the Captain of the 'Pelican'. [1 mark]
3. Tib was Drake's cabin boy. [1 mark]
4. Dickon had a lame leg. [1 mark]
5. Despite his leg, Dickon knew he could run and climb. [1 mark]

Try these
Assist children if they ask for help with vocabulary, first discussing what they think the words might mean. Ask children to write sentences to answer the questions, explaining their answers with reference to the text and their own experiences.

Suggested answers
1. *The second mate said that Dickon couldn't do the job because Dickon had a lame leg and wouldn't be able to climb the mainmast.* [example]
2. A 'doublet' is an old-fashioned waistcoat or jacket, 'lame' means weak or injured and 'widowed' means that a person's husband or wife has died. The words 'lame' and 'widowed' tell you that the life of Dickon and his family must be difficult. [4 marks]
3. The man who threw Dickon the bag was called John. He was Francis Drake's cousin. [2 marks]
4. John wanted Dickon to carry his bag onto the ship for him. [1 mark]
5. Evidence that the story is historical could include the fact that it is set on board a large sailing ship of a kind that no longer sails, and that it mentions 'Good Queen Bess', 'gold' instead of money and 'wearing a leather doublet'. [3 marks]

Now try these
Open-ended questions
1. Questions should be from Dickon's point of view and ask for details about the ship and the voyage. [3 marks max]
2. Diary entries should be from Tib's point of view and refer to details from the text. They should include Tib's feelings about the voyage and about Dickon not being given a job on the ship too. [3 marks max]
3. Pictures should be relevant to the extract, including details it mentions. They should feature Dickon either when he thinks he will be left behind or when he is running with John's bag. [3 marks max]

Support, embed & challenge

Support
Use Unit 9 Resource 1: Dickon's character to support children in exploring the character of Dickon further. Children should reread the text to find information that they can use in the profile. If the information is not easily located in the extract, discuss with the children what the answers could be, encouraging them to use their imagination.

Embed
Ask children to think about what clues an author can use to show the reader that a story is historical. Ask them to work in groups to find stories in the school library that are set in historical times, and to write a list of what the author includes.

Challenge
Use Unit 9 Resource 2: A story starts to guide children in planning their own adventure story openings. Encourage them to include a main character who thinks he/she will miss out on the adventure until the last moment, using the extract to give them ideas. As an extra challenge, ask the children to try to make their stories historical. Then ask the children to write their story openings.

Homework / Additional activities

Actual adventures
Ask children to research and find out about the real Sir Francis Drake and his adventures. Ask them to look particularly for the risks and hardships of his voyages. Ask: 'Would you have been keen to go sailing at that time?'

Collins Connect: Unit 9
Ask the children to complete Unit 9 (see Teach → Year 4 → Comprehension → Unit 9).

Unit 10: Playscript: 'In the Rue Bel Tesoro'

Overview

English curriculum objectives

- Listen to and discuss a wide range of fiction, poetry, plays, non-fiction and reference books or textbooks
- Read books that are structured in different ways and reading for a range of purposes
- Use dictionaries to check the meanings of words they have read
- Increase their familiarity with a wide range of books, including fairy stories, myths and legends, and retell some of these orally
- Identify themes and conventions in a wide range of books
- Prepare poems and playscripts to read aloud and to perform, showing understanding through intonation, tone, volume and action
- Discuss words and phrases that capture the reader's interest and imagination
- Check that the text makes sense to them, discussing their understanding and explaining the meaning of words in context
- Ask questions to improve their understanding of a text
- Draw inferences such as inferring characters' feelings, thoughts and motives from their actions, and justifying inferences with evidence
- Predict what might happen from details stated and implied
- Identify main ideas drawn from more than one paragraph and summarise these
- Identify how language, structure and presentation contribute to meaning
- Participate in discussion about both books that are read to them and those they can read for themselves, taking turns and listening to what others say

Treasure House resources

- Comprehension Skills Pupil Book 4, Unit 10, pages 34–36
- Collins Connect Treasure House Comprehension Year 4, Unit 10
- Photocopiable Unit 10, Resource 1: Finding the features, page 83
- Photocopiable Unit 10, Resource 2: Costumes and setting, page 84

Additional resources

- Dictionaries or the internet (optional)
- *In the Rue Bel Tesoro* by Lin Coghlan, whole text (optional)

Introduction

Teaching overview

In the Rue Bel Tesoro is a playscript containing four speaking parts: two children and two adults. The extract, from the beginning of the play, tells the story of two children (and their dog) who have to evade soldiers in order to board a train to find their grandmother. It is a play about children living in a country where soldiers are fighting and people are struggling to survive. The precise setting and time period of the story, however, remain non-specific.

Introduce the extract

Ask the children what they can remember about the form and conventions of playscripts. Take suggestions, and briefly discuss the layout of a playscript text. Then ask the children if they have ever read or heard stories set during wartime, and ask them to share their experiences.

Tell the children that, in this lesson, they will focus on one extract from a play about children trying to find their grandmother during a period of war. Then they will answer questions about it. Remind children that sometimes the answers to the questions will be clearly written in the extract, but that sometimes they may need to think a little harder and use their own ideas, supported by the text.

Ask the children to read the extract individually or in pairs. Ask them to note down any words they do not understand. Discuss unknown or unusual vocabulary before setting children to work answering the questions in the Pupil Book. Try to avoid discussing the content of the extract until after the children have answered the questions.

Unit 10: Playscript: 'In the Rue Bel Tesoro'

Pupil practice

Pupil Book pages 34–36

Get started

Children copy the sentences and complete them using information from the text.

Answers

1. Scene 1 is set in a busy <u>train</u> <u>station</u>. [1 mark]
2. Sasha and Omar's bag is stuffed with <u>belongings</u>. [1 mark]
3. The soldier checks everyone's <u>documents/papers</u>. [1 mark]
4. Fran is an <u>old</u> <u>woman</u>. [1 mark]
5. Omar tells Fran they have a <u>dog</u>, not a <u>baby</u>. [1 mark]

Try these

Assist children if they ask for help with vocabulary, first discussing what they think the words might mean. Ask children to write sentences to answer the questions, explaining their answers with reference to the text and their own experiences.

Suggested answers

1. *Valentine is in the pram.* [example]
2. Sasha wants to stay with Fran because she thinks that the soldiers don't stop older people with children as often. [1 mark]
3. Sasha is furious with Omar because he told Fran that they have a dog in the pram instead of a baby. (N.B. From the extract alone, it is not clear which is true.) [1 mark]
4. I think the children feel very frightened as they ran away from the soldier and could get into trouble. / I think the children feel annoyed that the soldier has tried to stop them because the baby doesn't have papers yet. [2 marks]
5. The text in brackets is stage directions. / The text in brackets tells you how the actors should move. [1 mark]

Now try these

Open-ended questions

1. Notes should draw out the facts from the extract (the children are at a train station in a country that is at war; there are a lot of soldiers around and everyone must carry papers). Look for relevant questions that are not answered by the extract. For example: What country is it? When is the play set? Is Valentine a dog or a baby? [3 marks max]
2. The message should be from Sasha's point of view, reacting to what happened at the station. Do not mark the answer based on letter-writing style, but on convincing relay of characterised emotion and the facts from the extract. [3 marks max]
3. Passages should contain all of the information from Scene 2 as a narrative, and should not retain any features of a playscript. [3 marks max]

Support, embed & challenge

Support

Use Unit 10 Resource 1: Finding the features to support children in familiarising themselves with the features of a playscript. Children should label the features with the terms supplied. They could also use coloured pens and highlighters to help with the identifications.

Embed

Use Unit 10 Resource 2: Costumes and setting to encourage children to think about how the play scene should look. They should note down costume ideas for each character, all the props needed and ideas about how the stage should look.

Challenge

Challenge children to act out the playscript and then to improvise the next part of the story. Ask them to think carefully about the setting (both the place and the time) as well as the children's characters and motivations. Ask: 'What will happen as the train stops?'

Homework / Additional activities

Plays on the page

Ask children to find other playscripts, and to look at their features closely. Ask them to study what things are similar to and what things are different from the features in the extract. Ask them to be prepared to share their findings with the class or a group.

Collins Connect: Unit 10

Ask the children to complete Unit 10 (see Teach → Year 4 → Comprehension → Unit 10).

Unit 11: Fiction: 'The Day the Helicopters Came'

Overview

English curriculum objectives

- Listen to and discuss a wide range of fiction, poetry, plays, non-fiction and reference books or textbooks
- Read books that are structured in different ways and reading for a range of purposes
- Use dictionaries to check the meanings of words they have read
- Increase their familiarity with a wide range of books, including fairy stories, myths and legends, and retell some of these orally
- Identify themes and conventions in a wide range of books
- Discuss words and phrases that capture the reader's interest and imagination
- Check that the text makes sense to them, discussing their understanding and explaining the meaning of words in context
- Ask questions to improve their understanding of a text
- Draw inferences such as inferring characters' feelings, thoughts and motives from their actions, and justifying inferences with evidence
- Predict what might happen from details stated and implied
- Identify main ideas drawn from more than one paragraph and summarise these
- Identify how language, structure and presentation contribute to meaning
- Participate in discussion about both books that are read to them and those they can read for themselves, taking turns and listening to what others say

Treasure House resources

- Comprehension Skills Pupil Book 4, Unit 11, pages 37–39
- Collins Connect Treasure House Comprehension Year 4, Unit 11
- Photocopiable Unit 11, Resource 1: The Vietnam War, page 85
- Photocopiable Unit 11, Resource 2: Character perspectives, page 86

Additional resources

- Dictionaries or the internet (optional)
- *The Day the Helicopters Came* by Rachel Anderson, whole text (optional)

Introduction

Teaching overview

The Day the Helicopters Came is a child's recollections of how frightening it was when an army invaded their village during the Vietnam War in the 1960s. The text provides an example of a first-person narrative written in a recount style.

Introduce the extract

Ask the children to think about why authors write stories. Collect suggestions, and draw out the idea that some stories are designed to share other people's experiences. Explain that *The Day the Helicopters Came* is a story that recalls how frightening it was for a young child during the Vietnam War. Tell the children that, although the story is fiction, it is representative of something that many children encounter if they live in times and areas affected by wars. If you wish, use Unit 11 Resource 1: The Vietnam War to give children some background information about the Vietnam War.

Tell the children that, in this lesson, they will focus on one extract from the story. Then they will answer questions about it. Remind children that sometimes the answers to the questions will be clearly written in the extract, but that sometimes they may need to think a little harder and use their own ideas, supported by the text.

Ask the children to read the extract individually or in pairs. Ask them to note down any words they do not understand. Discuss unknown or unusual vocabulary before setting children to work answering the questions in the Pupil Book. Try to avoid discussing the content of the extract until after the children have answered the questions.

Unit 11: Fiction: 'The Day the Helicopters Came'

Pupil practice

Pupil Book pages 37–39

Get started
Children copy the sentences and complete them using information from the text.

Answers
1. The girl's family had a cow because it could give them <u>milk</u>. [1 mark]
2. Her mother sent their spare rice and vegetables to the <u>market</u> in the <u>city</u>. [1 mark]
3. The helicopters landed on the <u>vegetable gardens</u>. [1 mark]
4. The men jumped out and <u>ran</u>. [1 mark]
5. The girl's mother <u>hurried</u> the family inside. [1 mark]

Try these
Assist children if they ask for help with vocabulary, first discussing what they think the words might mean. Ask children to write sentences to answer the questions, explaining their answers with reference to the text and their own experiences.

Suggested answers
1. *The girl's grandmother was 'in a trance' because she had spent three nights in the shelter. [example]*
2. The word 'succession' means a series of things and a 'lintel' is the beam above a door. In the setting of the extract, 'shells' are a kind of explosive bullet. [3 marks]
3. I think the soldiers felt frightened as they ran from the helicopter because the extract says they ran 'as though themselves afraid of being fired on'. / I think the soldiers felt aggressive/angry as they ran from the helicopter because of the way they spoke to the speaker's mother. [1 mark]
4. I think the girl knew the soldier in the doorway was frightened because he instinctively twitched his gun when her mother moved to snatch the baby. [1 mark]
5. I think the soldiers trampled on the vegetables because the helicopters didn't care about where they landed. / I think the soldiers trampled on the vegetables because they didn't notice where they were running. (NB: It will be unlikely that the children can justify an assertion that the soldiers are trampling the vegetables intentionally.) [1 mark]

Now try these
Open-ended questions
1. Sentences should be from the point of view of the girl's grandmother, and be consistent with the details of the extract. [3 marks max]
2. The eight lines of dialogue should be between the girl's mother and the soldier, and be appropriate to the events and the characters' feelings. [3 marks max]
3. Pictures and captions should be relevant to the extract, including details it mentions. [3 marks max]

Support, embed & challenge

Support
Use Unit 11 Resource 1: The Vietnam War to provide some background information about the Vietnam War. Read through the information with the children and discuss their reactions. Ask them to find facts relevant to the extract.

Embed
Use Unit 11 Resource 2: Character perspectives to encourage children to explore the different characters' perspectives. Ask them to read the story extract again, and to discuss and note down what the different characters were doing, saying, thinking and feeling during the extract.

Challenge
Challenge children to rewrite the extract as a diary entry by the mother.

Homework / Additional activities

What happened next?
Ask children to write a short continuation of the story. Ask: 'What do you think happened when the earthenware dish clattered on the floor?'

Collins Connect: Unit 11
Ask the children to complete Unit 11 (see Teach → Year 4 → Comprehension → Unit 11).

Unit 12: Poetry: Humans – Friends or Foes?

Overview

English curriculum objectives

- Listen to and discuss a wide range of fiction, poetry, plays, non-fiction and reference books or textbooks
- Read books that are structured in different ways and reading for a range of purposes
- Use dictionaries to check the meanings of words they have read
- Identify themes and conventions in a wide range of books
- Prepare poems and playscripts to read aloud and to perform, showing understanding through intonation, tone, volume and action
- Discuss words and phrases that capture the reader's interest and imagination
- Recognise some different forms of poetry
- Check that the text makes sense to them, discussing their understanding and explaining the meaning of words in context
- Ask questions to improve their understanding of a text
- Draw inferences such as inferring characters' feelings, thoughts and motives from their actions, and justifying inferences with evidence
- Identify how language, structure and presentation contribute to meaning
- Participate in discussion about both books that are read to them and those they can read for themselves, taking turns and listening to what others say

Treasure House resources

- Comprehension Skills Pupil Book 4, Unit 12, pages 40–42
- Collins Connect Treasure House Comprehension Year 4, Unit 12
- Photocopiable Unit 12, Resource 1: Describing the painting, page 87
- Photocopiable Unit 12, Resource 2: Making comparisons, page 88

Additional resources

- An image or video of an antelope
- Dictionaries or the internet (optional)
- Other poems and pictures that show relationships between people and animals (optional)

Introduction

Teaching overview

This unit introduces children to two contrasting depictions of humans' relationships with animals. It presents a poem called 'Kob Antelope', by an unknown Nigerian poet, and a Ragamala painting from medieval India. Both are about the tenuous relationship between people and animals, and both portray the potential for this relationship to be harmonious. The poem, however, also introduces the idea of humans as a threat.

Introduce the poem and painting

Before showing the children the poem or the painting, ask them to describe a deer. Encourage them to think about the way a deer looks and how it behaves. Note down their ideas as a mind map. Then ask if any of the children have seen an antelope. Again, note down any contributions. Then show the children an image or video of an antelope.

Tell the children that, in this lesson, they will focus on a poem and a painting that feature an antelope and a deer. Then they will answer questions about them. Remind children that sometimes the answers to the questions will be clearly written in the poem or seen in the painting, but that sometimes they may need to think a little harder and use their own ideas, supported by what they have read and can see.

Ask the children to read the poem and study the painting individually or in pairs. Ask them to note down anything they do not understand. Discuss unknown or unusual vocabulary before setting children to work answering the questions in the Pupil Book. Try to avoid discussing the content of the poem or painting until after the children have answered the questions.

Unit 12: Poetry: Humans – Friends or Foes?

Pupil practice

Pupil Book pages 40–42

Get started

Children copy the sentences and complete them using information from the text.

Answers

1. The poem is about a kob <u>antelope</u>. [1 mark]
2. There are five deer and one <u>woman/lady/girl</u> in the painting. [1 mark]
3. The painting is from <u>India</u> and the poem is from <u>Nigeria</u>. [1 mark]
4. The animal in the poem has <u>smooth</u> skin. [1 mark]
5. The animal in the poem has a <u>long</u> neck. [1 mark]

Try these

Assist children if they ask for help with vocabulary, first discussing what they think the words might mean. Ask children to write sentences to answer the questions, explaining their answers with reference to the text and their own experiences.

Suggested answers

1. *The hunter is the other character mentioned in the poem.* [example]
2. The antelope moves very carefully, trying to avoid danger. (Answers should paraphrase, not repeat, the words 'stepping cautiously'.) [1 mark]
3. I think the hunter wants to hurt/kill/trap/eat the antelope because that is what hunters do / because the hunter is described as 'greedy'. [1 mark]
4. I think that the poet likes/loves/wants to protect the antelope because the poem says the antelope is a 'creature to pet and spoil like a child'. [1 mark]
5. I think the woman and the deer in the painting like and trust one another. I think this because they are close together and looking at one another, and the woman is stretching out her hand to the deer gently. [1 mark]

Now try these

Open-ended questions

1. Similes from the poem: 'spoil like a child', 'eyes like a bird's' and 'head beautiful like carved wood'. [1 mark]
   The three new similes should provide reasonable comparison describing (elements of) the deer in the painting. [1 mark per simile]
2. Poems should be relevant to the details of the painting, regarding how the deer look and behave, be styled like 'Kob Antelope' and contain at least one new simile. [3 marks max]
3. Pictures should be relevant to the poem, including details it mentions, and attempts to use ideas from the painting. They may or may not feature the hunter and/or poet in addition to the antelope itself. [3 marks max]

Support, embed & challenge

Support

Use Unit 12 Resource 1: Describing the painting to support children in understanding the content of the painting. Read through the questions in the table and ask children to fill in their notes. Then ask children to use these ideas to write a paragraph to describe the painting.

Embed

Use Unit 12 Resource 2: Making comparisons to encourage children to compare and contrast the two sources. Ask children to answer the questions in the table by making notes, and then to write a short paragraph about which source they think is the most effective.

Challenge

Challenge children to write a poem and draw a contrasting picture to show a more negative relationship between animals and people.

Homework / Additional activities

Poem–picture pairs

Ask children to research and find another poem and painting that share a different subject. Ask them to be prepared to discuss the similarities and differences between the two sources' presentations of the subject.

Collins Connect: Unit 12

Ask the children to complete Unit 12 (see Teach → Year 4 → Comprehension → Unit 12).

Unit 13: Fiction: 'Angry Arthur' and Poetry: 'My Hair as Black as Dirty Coal'

Overview

English curriculum objectives

- Listen to and discuss a wide range of fiction, poetry, plays, non-fiction and reference books or textbooks
- Read books that are structured in different ways and reading for a range of purposes
- Use dictionaries to check the meanings of words they have read
- Increase their familiarity with a wide range of books, including fairy stories, myths and legends, and retell some of these orally
- Identify themes and conventions in a wide range of books
- Prepare poems and playscripts to read aloud and to perform, showing understanding through intonation, tone, volume and action
- Discuss words and phrases that capture the reader's interest and imagination
- Recognise some different forms of poetry
- Check that the text makes sense to them, discussing their understanding and explaining the meaning of words in context
- Ask questions to improve their understanding of a text
- Draw inferences such as inferring characters' feelings, thoughts and motives from their actions, and justifying inferences with evidence
- Predict what might happen from details stated and implied
- Identify main ideas drawn from more than one paragraph and summarise these
- Identify how language, structure and presentation contribute to meaning
- Participate in discussion about both books that are read to them and those they can read for themselves, taking turns and listening to what others say

Treasure House resources

- Comprehension Skills Pupil Book 4, Unit 13, pages 43–45
- Collins Connect Treasure House Comprehension Year 4, Unit 13
- Photocopiable Unit 13, Resource 1: Simile or metaphor?, page 89
- Photocopiable Unit 13, Resource 2: Feeling angry, page 90

Additional resources

- Dictionaries or the internet (optional)
- Other stories and poems that focus on exploring strong emotions (optional)

Introduction

Teaching overview

Angry Arthur is a metaphorical story about a boy who becomes angry when he is sent to bed. As his feelings of anger become more and more intense, they are described using increasingly powerful metaphors, making the earth explode and causing a 'universequake'. 'My Hair as Black as Dirty Coal' is a poem also focused on the main character's building anger, predominantly using similes to describe the emotion. The reason for the speaker's anger is supplied in fragments throughout the poem.

Introduce the text

Ask the children to try and describe how they feel when they are really angry. Ask what makes them feel angry, and encourage them to describe how anger feels in the stomach, head, mouth and eyes. Scribe children's ideas on the board.

Tell the children that, in this lesson, they will focus on an extract from a story and a poem that both explore how being angry feels. Then they will answer questions about them. Remind children that sometimes the answers to the questions will be clearly written in the extract or poem, but that sometimes they may need to think a little harder and use their own ideas, supported by the texts.

Ask the children to read the extract and poem individually or in pairs. Ask them to note down any words they do not understand. Discuss unknown or unusual vocabulary before setting children to work answering the questions in the Pupil Book. Try to avoid discussing the content of the extract or poem until after the children have answered the questions.

47

Unit 13: Fiction: 'Angry Arthur' and Poetry: 'My Hair as Black as Dirty Coal'

Pupil practice

Pupil Book pages 43–45

Get started
Children copy the sentences and complete them using information from the text.

Answers

1. Arthur's anger first became a <u>stormcloud</u> exploding thunder. [1 mark]
2. It then hurled rooftops and <u>chimneys</u> and <u>church</u> <u>spires</u>. [1 mark]
3. Arthur was angry because his mother said he couldn't watch a <u>TV programme</u>. [1 mark]
4. The poet was breathing like a <u>charging</u> <u>wild</u> bull. [1 mark]
5. His feet heat up ready to <u>kick</u> out. [1 mark]

Try these
Assist children if they ask for help with vocabulary, first discussing what they think the words might mean. Ask children to write sentences to answer the questions, explaining their answers with reference to the text and their own experiences.

Suggested answers

1. *The two extracts are similar because they are both about anger.* [example]
2. The words in brackets in the poem tell the reader the reason for the poet's anger. [1 mark]
3. Children should select four of the five similes in the poem: 'My hair as black as dirty coal', 'My eyes sizzle like fried eggs in a pan', 'My nose breathes heavily like a charging wild bull', 'My mouth breathing fire like a dragon' and 'I clench my fists hard like compressing a lemon'. [4 marks]
4. A metaphor is a word or phrase that describes one thing as though it is something else. [1 mark]
5. Hurricanes and typhoons are violent, windy storms. I think a universequake is like an earthquake that shakes the whole universe. These words help me to imagine how violent and destructive Arthur's anger is. [5 marks max]

Now try these
Open-ended questions

1. Answers should detect that writers use similes and metaphors to build up a clear picture. They help readers to visualise how angry the two children are. [3 marks max]
2. The three new similes should express the feelings (for example, guilt) that the poet's brother may be feeling. The poem reveals that the brother is responsible for the poet's anger as he kicked the poet's football over a fence. [3 marks max]
3. Paragraphs should use appropriate metaphors correctly to describe feeling happy. [3 marks max]

Support, embed & challenge

Support
Use Unit 13 Resource 1: Simile or metaphor? to support children in familiarising themselves with the nature of similes and metaphors. First, the children examine the examples from the poem. Then they label sentences to show whether they contain a simile or metaphor. (**Answers** 1. metaphor; 2. simile)

Embed
Use Unit 13 Resource 2: Feeling angry to encourage children to explore how they feel and behave when they are feeling angry. Prompt them to recall ideas scribed on the board at the beginning of the lesson. Then ask children to use their notes to write their own poems or short stories using powerful imagery.

Challenge
Challenge children to think about how the story and/or poem would be different if the subject was happiness rather than anger. Challenge them to adapt either the story or poem to make it about happiness, referring to their answers to 'Now try these' Question 3.

Homework / Additional activities

Feeling fearful
Ask children to write their own poems or short stories about the feeling of fear, using similes or metaphors where possible.

Collins Connect: Unit 13
Ask the children to complete Unit 13 (see Teach → Year 4 → Comprehension → Unit 13).

Unit 14: Non-fiction (information text): 'Feathered Record Breakers'

Overview

English curriculum objectives

- Listen to and discuss a wide range of fiction, poetry, plays, non-fiction and reference books or textbooks
- Read books that are structured in different ways and reading for a range of purposes
- Use dictionaries to check the meanings of words they have read
- Identify themes and conventions in a wide range of books
- Discuss words and phrases that capture the reader's interest and imagination
- Check that the text makes sense to them, discussing their understanding and explaining the meaning of words in context
- Ask questions to improve their understanding of a text
- Identify main ideas drawn from more than one paragraph and summarise these
- Identify how language, structure and presentation contribute to meaning
- Retrieve and record information from non-fiction
- Participate in discussion about both books that are read to them and those they can read for themselves, taking turns and listening to what others say

Treasure House resources

- Comprehension Skills Pupil Book 4, Unit 14, pages 46–48
- Collins Connect Treasure House Comprehension Year 4, Unit 14
- Photocopiable Unit 14, Resource 1: True or false?, page 91
- Photocopiable Unit 14, Resource 2: Bird fact file, page 92

Additional resources

- Dictionaries or the internet (optional)
- Other non-fiction texts about birds (optional)

Introduction

Teaching overview

'Feathered Record Breakers' provides an example of a non-fiction information text. It features characteristics such as subheadings, images, data, a clear layout and a formal, impersonal style.

Introduce the extract

Ask the children what facts they can tell you about birds. Write their ideas on the board.

Tell the children that, in this lesson, they will focus on an extract from an information text about bird record breakers. Then they will answer questions about it. Remind children that sometimes the answers to the questions will be clearly written in the extract, but that sometimes they may need to think a little harder and use their own ideas, supported by the text.

Ask the children to read the extract individually or in pairs. Ask them to note down any words they do not understand. Discuss unknown or unusual vocabulary before setting children to work answering the questions in the Pupil Book. Try to avoid discussing the content of the extract until after the children have answered the questions.

Unit 14: Non-fiction (information text): 'Feathered Record Breakers'

Pupil practice

Pupil Book pages 46–48

Get started
Children copy the sentences and complete them using information from the text.

Answers
1. The fastest flier is the <u>spine</u>-<u>tailed</u> <u>swift</u>. [1 mark]
2. Emperor penguins have dived over <u>250</u> <u>metres</u> deep. [1 mark]
3. The biggest bird alive is the <u>ostrich</u>. [1 mark]
4. A bee hummingbird weighs only <u>2</u> <u>grams</u>. [1 mark]
5. The roc weighed over <u>420</u> <u>kilograms</u>. [1 mark]

Try these
Assist children if they ask for help with vocabulary, first discussing what they think the words might mean. Ask children to write sentences to answer the questions, explaining their answers with reference to the text and their own experiences.

Suggested answers
1. *The ostrich holds two of these records: the biggest bird alive and the fastest runner.* [example]
2. The word 'wingspan' means the distance across a bird's wings from tip to tip. I think the bird in the extract with the smallest wingspan is the bee hummingbird. [2 marks]
3. The extract does not tell me whether the ostrich or the roc was taller. [1 mark]
4. I think the author included information about extinct birds because they are interesting. / I think the author included information about extinct birds because they break the records held by living birds. [1 mark]
5. The text uses subheadings to make the information clear and easy to understand. [1 mark]

Now try these
Open-ended questions
1. The three facts should be clear and written in the children's own words. They should not be taken from the extract. [3 marks max]
2. Paragraphs should contain facts about the chosen bird from the extract, and well-justified reasons why the children think it is the most interesting bird. [3 marks max]
3. Pictures and information boxes should be clear and accurate with regards to the facts given about ostriches and their eggs in the extract. They should include facts such as the ostrich's size, mass and egg size. [3 marks max]

Support, embed & challenge

Support
Use Unit 14 Resource 1: True or false? to support children in practising their reading memory skills. Ask them to try answering the questions without rereading the extract to find the answers. Then, when they have attempted the questions, they could reread the text to check their answers. (**Answers** 1. true, 2. false, 3. false, 4. true, 5. true, 6. false, 7. true, 8. false, 9. true, 10. false, 11. true, 12. true)

Embed
Use Unit 14 Resource 2: Bird fact file to encourage children to apply their learning by planning and writing their own fact files on birds of their choice. You may wish to provide time in the library or on the internet for children to research facts about their chosen birds.

Challenge
Challenge children to think about why people might be interested to learn facts about different birds, and why educating people about birds might be important (for example, to help with conservation). Ask children to discuss the topic in a group, and then to write paragraphs that explain their thoughts.

Homework / Additional activities

A class fact file
As a class, choose one bird not already studied over the course of the unit (for example, an owl or a kingfisher). Ask each child to research and find six interesting facts about this bird that they can share with the class. Create a new fact file using the class's responses.

Collins Connect: Unit 14
Ask the children to complete Unit 14 (see Teach → Year 4 → Comprehension → Unit 14).

Review unit 2: Non-fiction (information text): 'Extreme Sports'
Pupil Book pages 49–50

Get started
Children copy the sentences and complete them using information from the text.

Answers

1. *Extreme sportsmen and sportswomen <u>push themselves</u> to the limit.* [example]
2. If they climb high, they want to <u>climb</u> higher. [1 mark]
3. If they find <u>something</u> easy, they want to make it more difficult. [1 mark]
4. They want to challenge themselves, even if it means facing much greater <u>dangers</u> than in ordinary sports. [1 mark]
5. Parachutes were first used as a way of <u>escaping</u> safely from a hot-air balloon. [1 mark]

Try these
Assist children if they ask for help with vocabulary, first discussing what they think the words might mean. Ask children to write sentences to answer the questions, explaining their answers with reference to the text or their own experiences.

Suggested answers

1. Extreme sportsmen and sportswomen tend to be younger rather than older because most extreme sports are physically tough. [2 marks]
2. It is important for extreme sportsmen and sportswomen to have the qualities of fitness, skill, balance, training and experience. [2 marks]
3. Extreme sports involve all the action, adventure, thrills and heartaches of other sports, but with added risks, goals, difficulties, challenges and dangers. [2 marks]
4. The risks involved with airborne extreme sports are changes in the weather, the safety of the equipment and the danger of falling from a great height. (The risk posed by the weather is mentioned in the text and should be included. Other risks will be children's own suggestions.) [3 marks max]
5. I think someone might want to do a skydive because it would be exciting and an extreme experience. / I do not know why someone might want to do a skydive because it is risky and would be frightening. [1 mark]

Now try these
Open-ended questions

1. Any three accurate facts about extreme sports could be given. Award extra marks for facts not included in the extract. [3 marks]
2. Paragraphs should be formed of the child's own opinions, and should explain why the child feels she/he would or would not be well suited to doing extreme sports, and which sport (if any) she/he would like to try. [3 marks max]
3. Pictures should feature someone participating in any extreme sport. Labels and information boxes should be clear and accurate. [3 marks max]

Unit 15: Non-fiction (information text): 'What is the Sun?' and Poetry: 'What is the Sun?'

Overview

English curriculum objectives

- Listen to and discuss a wide range of fiction, poetry, plays, non-fiction and reference books or textbooks
- Read books that are structured in different ways and reading for a range of purposes
- Use dictionaries to check the meanings of words they have read
- Identify themes and conventions in a wide range of books
- Prepare poems and playscripts to read aloud and to perform, showing understanding through intonation, tone, volume and action
- Discuss words and phrases that capture the reader's interest and imagination
- Recognise some different forms of poetry
- Check that the text makes sense to them, discussing their understanding and explaining the meaning of words in context
- Ask questions to improve their understanding of a text
- Draw inferences such as inferring characters' feelings, thoughts and motives from their actions, and justifying inferences with evidence
- Predict what might happen from details stated and implied
- Identify main ideas drawn from more than one paragraph and summarise these
- Identify how language, structure and presentation contribute to meaning
- Retrieve and record information from non-fiction
- Participate in discussion about both books that are read to them and those they can read for themselves, taking turns and listening to what others say

Treasure House resources

- Comprehension Skills Pupil Book 4, Unit 15, pages 52–54
- Collins Connect Treasure House Comprehension Year 4, Unit 15
- Photocopiable Unit 15, Resource 1: The sun, page 93
- Photocopiable Unit 15, Resource 2: The moon, page 94

Additional resources

- Dictionaries or the internet (optional)
- Other pairs of non-fiction texts and poems about the same subject (optional)

Introduction

Teaching overview

This unit introduces children to two contrasting depictions of the sun. It presents one non-fiction information text and one poem on the topic, both with the title 'What is the Sun?'. The non-fiction text features characteristics such as technical data, a clear layout and a formal, impersonal style. By comparison, the poem is metaphorical, and explores subjective ideas of what the sun seems like to the poet.

Introduce the extract and poem

Ask the children to explain the differences between a poem and a non-fiction text. Note down their ideas on the board. Then ask them to describe the sun. Ask them to think about how the sun would be described in an information text and in a poem. Again, write the children's ideas on the board.

Tell the children that, in this lesson, they will focus on an extract from an information text and a poem that both describe the sun. Then they will answer questions about them. Remind children that sometimes the answers to the questions will be clearly written in the extract or poem, but that sometimes they may need to think a little harder and use their own ideas, supported by the texts.

Ask the children to read the extract and the poem individually or in pairs. Ask them to note down any words they do not understand. Discuss unknown or unusual vocabulary before setting children to work answering the questions in the Pupil Book. Try to avoid discussing the content of the extract or poem until after the children have answered the questions.

Unit 15: Non-fiction (information text): 'What is the Sun?' and Poetry: 'What is the Sun?'

Pupil practice

Pupil Book pages 52–54

Get started
Children copy the sentences and complete them using information from the text.

Answers

1. The sun is the nearest star to the <u>earth</u>. [1 mark]
2. The sun is quite a <u>small</u> star. [1 mark]
3. Without the sun we would have no <u>light</u> or <u>warmth</u>. [1 mark]
4. According to the poem, the Sun is a yellow <u>beach</u> <u>ball</u>. [1 mark]
5. According to the poem, the sky is like a sheet of <u>pale</u> <u>blue</u> <u>paper</u>. [1 mark]

Try these
Assist children if they ask for help with vocabulary, first discussing what they think the words might mean. Ask children to write sentences to answer the questions, explaining their answers with reference to the text and their own experiences.

Suggested answers

1. *The sun is important to us because there would be no light, warmth or life on earth without it. [example]*
2. There are five metaphors in the poem. There are no metaphors in the non-fiction text. [1 mark]
3. The sun is made of gas. I think this because the non-fiction text contains facts but the poem does not. [1 mark]
4. The poem describes the sun by using metaphors and impressions, while the non-fiction text includes only facts to describe it. [1 mark]
5. Neither of the texts tells me exactly how hot the sun is. I think the non-fiction text would be most likely to tell me because it is more likely to be exact instead of descriptive. [1 mark]

Now try these
Open-ended questions

1. Answers should attempt to distinguish the different motives behind the texts. For example, the non-fiction text intends to inform and educate the reader with facts, while the poem intends to entertain the reader and create vivid images in the imagination. [3 marks max]
2. Answers could choose either genre, but should include well-reasoned attempts to justify the preference and decision stated. [3 marks max]
3. The first picture and information boxes should be clear and accurate with regards to details from the information text, such as the bodies' sizes and the distance between them. The second picture should be relevant to the metaphorical details of the poem. [3 marks max]

Support, embed & challenge

Support
Use Unit 15 Resource 1: The sun to support children in describing the sun in different ways. Remind the children of the descriptions of the sun in the poem and in the information text, and the ideas they generated in the class discussion at the beginning of the lesson.

Embed
Use Unit 15 Resource 2: The moon to encourage children to apply ideas taken from the form and style of the source texts, and to use them to create their own texts about the moon. Enable them to conduct additional research in books or on the internet if possible.

Challenge
Challenge children to create a presentation about the sun using the information text and further research.

Homework / Additional activities

What is the moon?
Ask children to find out more about the moon. Ask them to compile a list of different facts using internet research and books, and to be prepared to present what they learn to groups or the class.

Collins Connect: Unit 15
Ask the children to complete Unit 15 (see Teach → Year 4 → Comprehension → Unit 15).

Unit 16: Poetry: 'Whale Alert'

Overview

English curriculum objectives

- Listen to and discuss a wide range of fiction, poetry, plays, non-fiction and reference books or textbooks
- Read books that are structured in different ways and reading for a range of purposes
- Use dictionaries to check the meanings of words they have read
- Identify themes and conventions in a wide range of books
- Prepare poems and playscripts to read aloud and to perform, showing understanding through intonation, tone, volume and action
- Discuss words and phrases that capture the reader's interest and imagination
- Recognise some different forms of poetry
- Check that the text makes sense to them, discussing their understanding and explaining the meaning of words in context
- Ask questions to improve their understanding of a text
- Draw inferences such as inferring characters' feelings, thoughts and motives from their actions, and justifying inferences with evidence
- Identify how language, structure and presentation contribute to meaning
- Participate in discussion about both books that are read to them and those they can read for themselves, taking turns and listening to what others say

Treasure House resources

- Comprehension Skills Pupil Book 4, Unit 16, pages 55–57
- Photocopiable Unit 16, Resource 1: Whale fact file, page 95
- Photocopiable Unit 16, Resource 2: A letter to whale hunters, page 96

Additional resources

- Dictionaries or the internet (optional)
- Other texts about whales and/or whale conservation (optional)

Introduction

Teaching overview

'Whale Alert' is a poem about whales. It uses a simple structure based on rhyming couplets. The speaker is a child who has been asked by a teacher to research an animal and chose the whale. Although reasonably light-hearted, the poem conveys an important message about the conservation and protection of whales.

Introduce the poem

Ask the children what they know about whales. Allow them to discuss the topic in pairs or small groups, and then ask them to feed back their thoughts as you scribe ideas on the board.

Tell the children that, in this lesson, they will focus on a poem about whales that is written from the perspective of a child learning about them. Then they will answer questions about it. Remind children that sometimes the answers to the questions will be clearly written in the poem, but that sometimes they may need to think a little harder and use their own ideas, supported by the text.

Ask the children to read the poem individually or in pairs. Ask them to note down any words they do not understand. Discuss unknown or unusual vocabulary before setting children to work answering the questions in the Pupil Book. Try to avoid discussing the content of the poem until after the children have answered the questions.

Pupil practice

Pupil Book pages 55–57

Get started

Children copy the sentences and complete them using information from the text.

Answers

1. Teacher said, "<u>Research</u> an animal, in the sea, the air, the ground." [1 mark]
2. The whale's got a song that could <u>melt</u> <u>your</u> <u>heart</u>. [1 mark]
3. Whales live on <u>fishy</u> <u>things</u> smaller'n me and you. [1 mark]
4. In just <u>50</u> <u>years</u>, two million whales have died. [1 mark]
5. But whales would be <u>happier</u> living in the sea. [1 mark]

Unit 16: Poetry: 'Whale Alert'

Try these
Assist children if they ask for help with vocabulary, first discussing what they think the words might mean. Ask children to write sentences to answer the questions, explaining their answers with reference to the text and their own experiences.

Suggested answers

1. *The teacher asked the speaker to research an animal.* [example]
2. According to the poem, whales can hear extremely well. [1 mark]
3. According to the poem, whales are hunted for their meat, oil and bones. [3 marks max]
4. I think the poet cares for whales a lot, because she describes them in a positive way / because she says she's sad to know that people treat the whale so badly. [3 marks max]
5. I think the poet is trying to share the message that whales don't deserve to be hunted by humans, and should be left alone and free. [3 marks max]

Now try these
Open-ended questions

1. Sentences should be from a whale's point of view, and may or may not consider how it might feel to live in the ocean, to communicate the way a whale does and/or to be hunted. [3 marks max]
2. Rhyming words: 'ground'/'found'; 'smart'/'heart'; 'smell'/'well'; 'say'/'away'; 'click'/'quick'; 'chew'/'you'; 'know'/'so'; 'bone'/'alone'; 'died'/'side'; 'whales'/'tales'; 'be'/'sea'. The four new lines should be about whales and be two rhyming couplets. [2 marks]
3. Posters should be aimed at raising awareness of the danger faced by whales and be relevant to the information in the poem. [3 marks max]

Support, embed & challenge

Support
Use Unit 16 Resource 1: Whale fact file to support children in looking at the information in the poem more closely. Ask the children to use the poem to fill in the fact file.

Embed
Use Unit 16 Resource 2: A letter to whale hunters to encourage children to write a letter to the company director of an imaginary company that sells products made from whale meat, bone and/or oil. Ask children to refer to the bullet points on the worksheet as they plan and write their letter.

Challenge
Challenge children to rewrite the poem as though the poet had chosen a different animal to research. Ask them to find and compile their facts before making a start on the poem itself, using 'Whale Alert' as a model.

Homework / Additional activities

More about whales
Ask children to do further research into whales and the threats facing them. Ask them to compile fact files or to be prepared to present their information to the class.

Unit 17: Fiction (modern): 'Cave Wars'

Overview

English curriculum objectives

- Listen to and discuss a wide range of fiction, poetry, plays, non-fiction and reference books or textbooks
- Read books that are structured in different ways and reading for a range of purposes
- Use dictionaries to check the meanings of words they have read
- Increase their familiarity with a wide range of books, including fairy stories, myths and legends, and retell some of these orally
- Identify themes and conventions in a wide range of books
- Discuss words and phrases that capture the reader's interest and imagination
- Check that the text makes sense to them, discussing their understanding and explaining the meaning of words in context
- Ask questions to improve their understanding of a text
- Draw inferences such as inferring characters' feelings, thoughts and motives from their actions, and justifying inferences with evidence
- Predict what might happen from details stated and implied
- Identify main ideas drawn from more than one paragraph and summarise these
- Identify how language, structure and presentation contribute to meaning
- Participate in discussion about both books that are read to them and those they can read for themselves, taking turns and listening to what others say

Treasure House resources

- Comprehension Skills Pupil Book 4, Unit 17, pages 58–60
- Photocopiable Unit 17, Resource 1: Now and then, page 97
- Photocopiable Unit 17, Resource 2: Us and them, page 98

Additional resources

- Dictionaries or the internet (optional)
- *Cave Wars* by Gillian Cross, whole text (optional)

Introduction

Teaching overview

Cave Wars is a story about two children, Tom and Ruby, who live at the seaside and enjoy playing in their 'secret' caves – until they find that a 'gang' of other children has taken over their space. The extract is taken from the beginning of the story, so includes a description of the caves and the scenario, as well as dialogue. It is useful for discussing the characters' feelings and motivations as well as making predictions about how the story might develop.

Introduce the extract

Ask the children if any of them has ever had trouble when meeting children new to their home area or school. Ask if they found the newcomers threatening in any way, and encourage them to share their experiences with the group. Guide the children in being understanding of other children when any difficult situations are discussed. (The opposite situation, the difficulties of being new to an area oneself, will be discussed in Unit 18.)

Tell the children that, in this lesson, they will focus on an extract from a story about two children who suddenly find the caves where they play have been taken over by children they don't know. Then they will answer questions about it. Remind children that sometimes the answers to the questions will be clearly written in the extract, but that sometimes they may need to think a little harder and use their own ideas, supported by the text.

Ask the children to read the extract individually or in pairs. Ask them to note down any words they do not understand. Discuss unknown or unusual vocabulary before setting children to work answering the questions in the Pupil Book. Try to avoid discussing the content of the extract until after the children have answered the questions.

Unit 17: Fiction (modern): 'Cave Wars'

Pupil practice

Pupil Book pages 58–60

Get started

Children copy the sentences and complete them using information from the text.

Answers

1. Tom and Ruby lived at the <u>seaside</u>, in a house near the beach. [1 mark]
2. The big one was higher up, behind a <u>heap of rocks</u>. [1 mark]
3. One wet winter afternoon, Tom and Ruby <u>decided</u> to make a camp in the big cave. [1 mark]
4. The boys nodded and pulled <u>horrible faces</u>. [1 mark]
5. There was a piece of old <u>board</u> lying on the beach. [1 mark]

Try these

Assist children if they ask for help with vocabulary, first discussing what they think the words might mean. Ask children to write sentences to answer the questions, explaining their answers with reference to the text and their own experiences.

Suggested answers

1. *Tom and Ruby took a rug and some sausages to the beach.* *[example]*
2. The little cave was low down in the cliff, hidden in the bushes. The big one was higher up, behind a heap of rocks. [1 mark]
3. Tom and Ruby played in the secret caves in the winter. They didn't play in them all year round because, in the summer, there were lots of people around. [1 mark]
4. Ruby did not like the other children in the cave. I know this because the extract says that Ruby wanted to fight them and was very, very angry. [2 marks]
5. I don't think it was fair for Ruby to call the bigger cave 'our cave', because the cave does not belong to her and Tom, and can be used by anyone. / I do think it was fair for Ruby to call the bigger cave 'our cave', because she and Tom live nearby and always play there. [2 marks]

Now try these

Open-ended questions

1. Sentences should be from Tom's perspective and respond to the confrontation with the children in the cave. [3 marks max]
2. Paragraphs should continue the story and explain Tom's idea for using a piece of old board to drive the new children away. [3 marks max]
3. Pictures should be relevant to the extract, including details it mentions. [3 marks max]

Support, embed & challenge

Support

Use Unit 17 Resource 1: Now and then to support children in understanding the motivations of Ruby and Tom. They complete two diary entries as though Ruby or Tom has written them before and after the new children arrive.

Embed

Use Unit 17 Resource 2: Us and them to encourage children to consider the new children's point of view as well as that of Ruby and Tom. They complete two diary entries, one as though Ruby or Tom has written it, and one as though a gang member has written it.

Challenge

Challenge children to discuss what may happen next in the story. Ask children to consider how the difficult situation could be worked out best, as well as whether or not they think this will happen. Suggest that they record their predictions as notes to present to the rest of the class.

Homework / Additional activities

A special place

Ask children to write short paragraphs about a special place where they like to go to or play. Ask them to imagine they found some other children in that place. Encourage them to consider both what they *would* do or say and what they *should* do or say.

Unit 18: Playscript: 'Sophie's Rules'

Overview

English curriculum objectives

- Listen to and discuss a wide range of fiction, poetry, plays, non-fiction and reference books or textbooks
- Read books that are structured in different ways and reading for a range of purposes
- Use dictionaries to check the meanings of words they have read
- Increase their familiarity with a wide range of books, including fairy stories, myths and legends, and retell some of these orally
- Identify themes and conventions in a wide range of books
- Prepare poems and playscripts to read aloud and to perform, showing understanding through intonation, tone, volume and action
- Discuss words and phrases that capture the reader's interest and imagination
- Check that the text makes sense to them, discussing their understanding and explaining the meaning of words in context
- Ask questions to improve their understanding of a text
- Draw inferences such as inferring characters' feelings, thoughts and motives from their actions, and justifying inferences with evidence
- Predict what might happen from details stated and implied
- Identify main ideas drawn from more than one paragraph and summarise these
- Identify how language, structure and presentation contribute to meaning
- Participate in discussion about both books that are read to them and those they can read for themselves, taking turns and listening to what others say

Treasure House resources

- Comprehension Skills Pupil Book 4, Unit 18, pages 61–63
- Photocopiable Unit 18, Resource 1: Sophie and Dana, page 99
- Photocopiable Unit 18, Resource 2: Different characters, page 100

Additional resources

- Dictionaries or the internet (optional)
- *Sophie's Rules* by Keith West, whole text (optional)

Introduction

Teaching overview

Sophie's Rules is a playscript that tells the story of a girl, Dana, who attempts to fit in with her peers at a new school. Dana is keen to make friends with Sophie and her fellow classmates, but Sophie responds with bullying behaviour. As well as providing a model of a playscript format, this story provides plenty of thought-provoking content about personal and social issues. The scene in the extract contains four speaking parts.

Introduce the extract

Remind the children of the topic discussed in Unit 17 (if completed). Ask the children if any of them has ever been in the opposite position, and had trouble when they have been new to a home area or school. Then ask them what they know about bullying. Guide the children in being understanding of other children when any difficult situations are discussed.

Tell the children that, in this lesson, they will focus on an extract from a playscript about a girl who tries to make friends at a new school. Then they will answer questions about it. Remind children that sometimes the answers to the questions will be clearly written in the extract, but that sometimes they may need to think a little harder and use their own ideas, supported by the text.

Ask the children to read the extract individually or in pairs. Ask them to note down any words they do not understand. Discuss unknown or unusual vocabulary before setting children to work answering the questions in the Pupil Book. Try to avoid discussing the content of the extract until after the children have answered the questions.

Unit 18: Playscript: 'Sophie's Rules'

Pupil practice

Pupil Book pages 61–63

Get started
Children copy the sentences and complete them using information from the text.

Answers
1. Dana's new to <u>Deepvale</u> School. [1 mark]
2. She notices Sophie, Anna and <u>Jade</u>. [1 mark]
3. I can tell you're not from <u>round here</u>. [1 mark]
4. We don't like people from <u>Wordsworth</u> Crescent. [1 mark]
5. Why aren't you in <u>school uniform</u>, like us? [1 mark]

Try these
Assist children if they ask for help with vocabulary, first discussing what they think the words might mean. Ask children to write sentences to answer the questions, explaining their answers with reference to the text and their own experiences.

Suggested answers
1. *Anna says that Dana can sit with them if she likes.* [example]
2. Sophie says she can tell Dana isn't from 'round here' because Dana's different. [1 mark]
3. Sophie feels annoyed/angry/aggressive when Anna invites Dana to sit down. I know this because the stage directions say she scowls. [2 marks]
4. I do not think Sophie, Anna and Jade all feel the same way about Dana, because Anna asks Dana to sit with them before Sophie starts being mean to her. / I do think Sophie, Anna and Jade all feel the same way about Dana, because they all say they don't like people from Wordsworth Crescent. [2 marks]
5. I can tell this is a playscript because it is made up of dialogue with no speech marks. Each speaker is stated at the beginning of the line, followed by the speech. There are stage directions in brackets. The extract starts with the heading 'Scene 1'. [3 marks max]

Now try these
Open-ended questions
1. Diary extracts should be from Dana's point of view, reacting to the conversation in the extract. The extracts may also consider how her feelings may have changed by the time she writes the diary entry. [3 marks max]
2. Paragraphs should explain what may happen next, and be relevant to the details of the extract. They should consider Dana's next actions and may relate these to children's own points of view. [3 marks max]
3. Pictures should be relevant to the extract, including details it mentions. Attempts should be made to show facial expressions and body language to express the character's feelings. [3 marks max]

Support, embed & challenge

Support
Use Unit 18 Resource 1: Sophie and Dana to support children in understanding the differences between Sophie and Dana. They complete the profile template using the extract, and are then asked to speculate on each girl's motivations.

Embed
Use Unit 18 Resource 2: Different characters to encourage children to recognise and consider each of the characters in the extract, using the text to give evidence for their opinions on each character.

Challenge
Challenge children to improvise what may happen next in the play. Ask children to consider how the difficult situation could be worked out best, as well as whether or not they think this will happen. Suggest that they then perform their predictions for the rest of the class, or use them as the start of a wider discussion.

Homework / Additional activities

A letter of advice
Ask the children to write a letter to either Dana or Sophie, giving their advice on how to deal with the difficult situation.

Unit 19: Non-fiction (information text): 'Black Holes'

Overview

English curriculum objectives

- Listen to and discuss a wide range of fiction, poetry, plays, non-fiction and reference books or textbooks
- Read books that are structured in different ways and reading for a range of purposes
- Use dictionaries to check the meanings of words they have read
- Identify themes and conventions in a wide range of books
- Discuss words and phrases that capture the reader's interest and imagination
- Check that the text makes sense to them, discussing their understanding and explaining the meaning of words in context
- Ask questions to improve their understanding of a text
- Identify main ideas drawn from more than one paragraph and summarise these
- Identify how language, structure and presentation contribute to meaning
- Retrieve and record information from non-fiction
- Participate in discussion about both books that are read to them and those they can read for themselves, taking turns and listening to what others say

Treasure House resources

- Comprehension Skills Pupil Book 4, Unit 19, pages 64–66
- Photocopiable Unit 19, Resource 1: True or false?, page 101
- Photocopiable Unit 19, Resource 2: Once upon a time, in space ..., page 102

Additional resources

- Dictionaries or the internet (optional)
- *Black Holes* by Anna Claybourne, whole text (optional)

Introduction

Teaching overview

'Black Holes' is a non-fiction information text, from the book *Black Holes* by Anna Claybourne. It has typical features such as subheadings and an impersonal narrative style. The information in the extract explains, in child-friendly language, about the discovery of black holes and what they are.

Introduce the text

Ask the children if they know anything about black holes (such as where they are found). If they do, invite them to share their knowledge with the class.

Tell the children that, in this lesson, they will focus on an extract from an information text about black holes. Then they will answer questions about it. Remind children that sometimes the answers to the questions will be clearly written in the text, but that sometimes they may need to think a little harder and use their own ideas, supported by the text.

Ask the children to read the text individually or in pairs. Ask them to note down any words they do not understand. Discuss unknown or unusual vocabulary before setting children to work answering the questions in the Pupil Book. Try to avoid discussing the content of the text until after the children have answered the questions.

Unit 19: Non-fiction (information text): 'Black Holes'

Pupil practice

Pupil Book pages 64–66

Get started
Children copy the sentences and complete them using information from the text.

Answers
1. Telescopes were <u>invented</u> in 1609. [1 mark]
2. Galileo discovered that the <u>Milky Way</u> was made of billions of stars. [1 mark]
3. John Michell wrote about strange objects that <u>swallowed</u> light. [1 mark]
4. Black holes aren't <u>actually</u> holes. [1 mark]
5. A black hole is like a tiny, invisible <u>point</u> in <u>space</u>. [1 mark]

Try these
Assist children if they ask for help with vocabulary, first discussing what they think the words might mean. Ask children to write sentences to answer the questions, explaining their answers with reference to the text and their own experiences.

Suggested answers
1. *Galileo used his telescope to look at Saturn's rings and Jupiter's moons.* [example]
2. In the 20th century, scientists discovered signs that dark stars / black holes really do exist. [1 mark]
3. John Michell said you could not see dark stars, but that they made other stars move in a strange way. [1 mark]
4. I do think that comparing a black hole to a powerful plughole helps the reader to understand what a black hole is like, as it helps to create an image of things being pulled into the black hole. / I do not think that comparing a black hole to a powerful plughole helps the reader to understand what a black hole is like, as the text says that black holes are not actually holes. [1 mark]
5. I think it might be difficult to find out more about black holes because spaceships and astronauts can't get close to them without disappearing into them. [1 mark]

Now try these
Open-ended questions
1. Sentences should be from Galileo's perspective, reacting to his discoveries of Saturn's rings and Jupiter's moons, and the fact that the Milky Way is made of billions of stars. [3 marks max]
2. The three facts should be in the children's own words. They may or may not be new facts learned through extra research. [3 marks max]
3. Timelines should show events from the extract noted in chronological order:
   - 1609: Telescopes were invented.
   - Galileo discovered that the Milky Way is made of billions of stars.
   - 1784: John Michell wrote about strange objects in space that swallowed light.
   - 20th century: Scientists found signs that dark stars / black holes really do exist.

   They may or may not also show other astronomical events learned through extra research. [3 marks max]

Support, embed & challenge

Support
Use Unit 19 Resource 1: True or false? to support children in practising their reading memory skills. Ask them to try answering the questions without rereading the extract to find the answers. Then, when they have attempted the questions, they could reread the text to check their answers. (**Answers** 1. true, 2. true, 3. false, 4. false, 5. true, 6. false, 7. false, 8. true, 9. true, 10. false, 11. false, 12. true)

Embed
Ask children to create a poster or presentation about black holes that they could use to explain the information they have learned to someone else.

Challenge
Challenge children to use Unit 19 Resource 2: Once upon a time, in space … to use the factual information in a creative way. The children answer the questions in the planning grid before starting to write short stories about a team of astronauts who come across a black hole while on a space mission.

Homework / Additional activities

Questioning space
Ask children to think about what else they would like to know about black holes. Ask them to compile a list of ten questions that are not answered by the extract, and that they could research.

Unit 20: Fiction (modern): 'Tiger Dead! Tiger Dead!'

Overview

English curriculum objectives

- Listen to and discuss a wide range of fiction, poetry, plays, non-fiction and reference books or textbooks
- Read books that are structured in different ways and reading for a range of purposes
- Use dictionaries to check the meanings of words they have read
- Increase their familiarity with a wide range of books, including fairy stories, myths and legends, and retell some of these orally
- Identify themes and conventions in a wide range of books
- Discuss words and phrases that capture the reader's interest and imagination
- Check that the text makes sense to them, discussing their understanding and explaining the meaning of words in context
- Ask questions to improve their understanding of a text
- Draw inferences such as inferring characters' feelings, thoughts and motives from their actions, and justifying inferences with evidence
- Predict what might happen from details stated and implied
- Identify main ideas drawn from more than one paragraph and summarise these
- Identify how language, structure and presentation contribute to meaning
- Participate in discussion about both books that are read to them and those they can read for themselves, taking turns and listening to what others say

Treasure House resources

- Comprehension Skills Pupil Book 4, Unit 20, pages 67–69
- Photocopiable Unit 20, Resource 1: Tiger's plan, page 103
- Photocopiable Unit 20, Resource 2: Anansi's plan, page 104

Additional resources

- Dictionaries or the internet (optional)
- *Tiger Dead! Tiger Dead!* by Grace Nichols, whole text (optional)

Introduction

Teaching overview

Tiger Dead! Tiger Dead! is an amusing story from the Caribbean about a tiger who decides he would like to get rid of all the other animals and keep the jungle for himself. He devises a plan, but he doesn't realise that clever Anansi has overheard him and has his own plans to foil the tiger.

Introduce the extract

Ask the children if any of them has ever heard a story featuring a character called Anansi. Explain that Anansi is a half-spider, half-man character who appears in many Caribbean tales: he is a clever trickster, who often outsmarts mean or selfish characters, and brings them to justice – often while benefitting himself.

Tell the children that, in this lesson, they will focus on an extract from one story that features Anansi. Then they will answer questions about it. Remind children that sometimes the answers to the questions will be clearly written in the extract, but that sometimes they may need to think a little harder and use their own ideas, supported by the text.

Ask the children to read the extract individually or in pairs. Ask them to note down any words they do not understand. Discuss unknown or unusual vocabulary before setting children to work answering the questions in the Pupil Book. Try to avoid discussing the content of the extract until after the children have answered the questions.

Unit 20: Fiction (modern): 'Tiger Dead! Tiger Dead!'

Pupil practice

Pupil Book pages 67–69

Get started
Children copy the sentences and complete them using information from the text.

Answers
1. One day Tiger was <u>strolling</u> through the forest. [1 mark]
2. Times were <u>hard</u> and suddenly an idea came to Tiger's head. [1 mark]
3. Tiger didn't see <u>Anansi himself</u> sitting on top of a palm tree. [1 mark]
4. Anansi had <u>listened</u> to every single word. [1 mark]
5. Well, as soon as Tiger got home he told his <u>wife</u> about the <u>plan</u> he had to become king of the jungle. [1 mark]

Try these
Assist children if they ask for help with vocabulary, first discussing what they think the words might mean. Ask children to write sentences to answer the questions, explaining their answers with reference to the text and their own experiences.

Suggested answers
1. *Tiger kept stopping every few moments to admire his stripy face in a stream.* [example]
2. The idea that came to Tiger's head was that it would be nice to have the forest all to himself. [1 mark]
3. Tiger fell in love with the idea. [1 mark]
4. Anansi is troublesome and tricky. I think he is likely to try and stop Tiger from completing his plan because the extract says he was the last person Tiger would have wanted to overhear him. [3 marks]
5. I would describe Tiger's personality as vain, selfish, crafty, unfriendly and mean. [2 marks max]

Now try these
Open-ended questions
1. Sentences should be from the point of view of Tiger's wife, responding to hearing Tiger's idea and plan. [3 marks max]
2. Retellings should contain all of the details in the extract, narrated from Anansi's point of view. [3 marks max]
3. Pictures and speech bubbles should be relevant to the extract and the details it mentions. [3 marks max]

Support, embed & challenge

Support
Use Unit 20 Resource 1: Tiger's plan to support children in clarifying what Tiger's plan is, and what he hopes to achieve.

Embed
Use Unit 20 Resource 2: Anansi's plan to encourage children to consider what Anansi's plan might be, in reaction to what he has learned.

Challenge
Challenge children to discuss what may happen next in the story. Ask them to consider how the different characters' plans might work out, and what lessons might be learned. Suggest that they record their predictions as notes to present to the rest of the class.

Homework / Additional activities

Another Anansi story
Ask children to research and find other stories about Anansi to share with the class. Ask: 'What aspects of the stories stay the same?'

Review unit 3: Poetry: 'Feeding the Ducks' — Pupil Book pages 70–71

Get started
Children copy the sentences and complete them using information from the text.

Answers

1. We're off to <u>feed</u> the <u>ducks</u>. [1 mark]
2. Hear them <u>quacking</u> in the <u>rain</u>. [1 mark]
3. What <u>shall</u> we feed the <u>ducks</u>? [1 mark]
4. Soggy <u>bread</u> means <u>tummy</u> pain. [1 mark]
5. Snails and slugs and <u>insects</u>,
   Worms and <u>hard</u>-<u>boiled</u> <u>eggs</u>. [1 mark]

Try these
Assist children if they ask for help with vocabulary, first discussing what they think the words might mean. Ask children to write sentences to answer the questions, explaining their answers with reference to the text or their own experiences.

Suggested answers

1. *The speaker is going to feed ducks.* [example]
2. The poem suggests that ducks should eat snails, slugs, insects, worms, hard-boiled eggs, turnip-tops, lettuce, acorns, seed and grain. [1 mark]
3. Ducks shouldn't eat soggy bread because it causes them to have tummy pain / because they can't digest it properly. [2 marks]
4. I think a young girl/boy is going to feed the ducks with his/her family and/or friends. (Answers should grasp that the speaker of the poem is likely to be a child, and that he or she is not going to feed the ducks alone: the active pronoun used in the poem is 'we'.) [2 marks]
5. The part of the poem that is repeated most often are the words 'the ducks'. In addition, in verses 1, 2 and 4, the first line is repeated as that verse's third line. The effect of this repetition on the reader is to emphasise the importance of the ducks to the speaker of the poem, and to give a sense of the excitement they cause. It also gives the verses a chant-like, sing-song effect that again adds to the poem's sense of joy and excitement. [3 marks max]

Now try these
Open-ended questions

1. Sentences should be from the point of view of the speaker of the poem, and express how he or she feels about the ducks. Answers should refer to the speaker's concern for health of the ducks, and the care taken in choosing foods that will not make them ill. [3 marks]
2. Rhyming words: 'rain'/'pain'/'grain'/'again'. [1 mark]

   The two new verses should be about the ducks, and contain four lines each. Their last lines should rhyme with one another, and their first three lines may or may not repeat words (possible rhyme schemes: AAAB AAAB, ABCD EFGD or ABCD EEED). [3 marks max]
3. Pictures should be relevant to the extract, including details it mentions. They should feature the ducks being fed as described in the poem (specifically, not on bread). [3 marks max]

Unit 1 Resource 1

Plan a visit

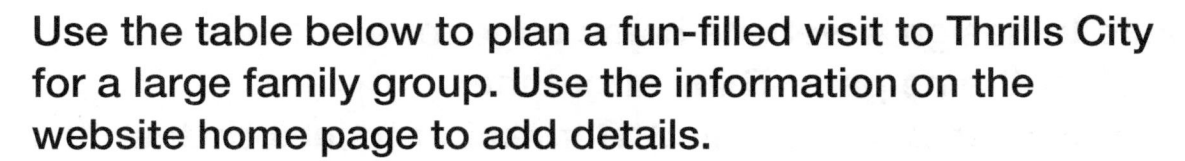

Use the table below to plan a fun-filled visit to Thrills City for a large family group. Use the information on the website home page to add details.

Ideas to get you started:

- How will you travel there?
- How many days will you stay?
- How many nights will you stay in the hotel?
- What time will you enter the park?
- Which ride will you go to first?
- Will different family members prefer different activities?

Day and time	Activity	Who will enjoy this most?

Unit 1 Resource 2

Design a website

Use the template to design a website home page for a campsite or another theme park. Think about the information your users may want to find. Remember to include the tabs you will need to take your users to different web pages.

Tabs					
Header					
Major attractions					
Attraction information and picture					
Special offers					
Practical information					

Unit 2 Resource 1

Similes

A simile compares one thing to another thing. Similes usually use 'as' or 'like' to compare the two things.

For example: 'We plant it like a flower in the field.'

First, draw lines to complete the four similes found in 'I Love Our Orange Tent'.

Then draw lines to complete the other similes by making good comparisons.

We plant it …	like yellow honey
My tent flaps …	like a log
It pours in …	like diamonds
It glows …	like roses
The snow glitters …	like a ballerina
She dances …	like a flower in the field
He ran home …	like a galloping horse
They fought …	like a flying bird
Your cheeks are red …	like gold
I slept …	like cats and dogs

© HarperCollinsPublishers Ltd 2017

67

Unit 2 Resource 2

My descriptive poem

Plan a poem in a similar style to 'I Love Our Orange Tent', to describe an interesting experience. Remember to think about the sights, smells, noises, tastes and feelings. If you can, include some similes too.

First, choose the experience you will describe, and use it in the title of your poem.

I Love _____

By _____

Sights	
Smells	
Noises	
Tastes	
Feelings	
Ideas for similes	

Now start writing your poem!

Unit 3 Resource 1

Comparing animals

Complete the second column in the table with information about the new-born donkey. Then choose two different animals and complete the table.

Animal	New-born donkey		
What does it look like?			
Where does it live?			
How does it move and behave?			
How do you think it feels?			
How do you feel about it?			

Unit 3 Resource 2

My new-born animal poem

Use the structure of 'The Donkey' to help you write a poem about a new-born animal of your choice. Use the same rhyme structure, and write at least two verses with eight short lines each.

Be sure to describe details of how your subject looks, moves and behaves. You could use the structure below.

Verse 1
Lines 1–4: Introduce the animal.
Lines 5–8: Describe the animal.
Verse 2
Lines 1–4: Describe how the animal moves and behaves.
Lines 5–8: Describe how you think the animal feels. You could also describe how you feel about it.

_____

By _____

Verse 1   Verse 2

Unit 4 Resource 1

Find the facts

Fill in the table by finding the information in the report of 'The Accident'.

What happened?	
When did it happen?	
Where did it happen?	
Why did it happen?	
How did it happen?	
Who was involved?	
What did the person interviewed say?	
How did they feel?	

© HarperCollins*Publishers* Ltd 2017

Unit 4 Resource 2

Tell the story

Rewrite the events in the report as a narrative story. Remember that narratives can have more description and dialogue than a newspaper report usually does.

Use the template prompts to help you.

One day, Mrs Wills went to visit her sister, who was ill. …
Mrs Wills and the Labrador left the house for their walk. …
Suddenly, the dog saw a duck on the icy river. …
The people walking nearby rushed to the river bank. …

Unit 5 Resource 1

A letter from the pilot

Imagine you are the pilot. Imagine how you must feel after being rescued. Use the template below to write a letter to Meena and Stacey, thanking them for phoning Air-Sea Rescue. You could use the sentence starters below.

Sea Harbour Hospital
Ocean Road
Littlecombe-on-Sea
Devon

Date: _____

Dear Meena and Stacey,

Thank you so much...

If you hadn't seen me falling,...

I am now...

I feel...

Many thanks again!

Unit 5 Resource 2

A news report

Write your own news report about the events in the diary entries. Remember to give details that describe what happened, when, where, why and to whom.

THE DAILY NEWS

By

Unit 6 Resource 1

Making decisions

Think about the decisions made by the Turtle and the Eagle. How might things have worked out differently?

The Turtle

What did the Turtle decide he wanted?	
Why did he make that decision?	
What would have happened if he had made a different decision?	

The Eagle

What did the Eagle decide to do?	
Why did he make that decision?	
What would have happened if he had made a different decision?	

Unit 6 Resource 2

A story of advice

Think of a piece of advice that someone has given you in the past. You could use 'be careful what you wish for' or 'you don't know what you've got until it's gone'.

Discuss with a partner how this piece of advice could become a story. Then use the grid below to plan your own short story, using different animal characters, and include your piece of advice as its moral.

What piece of advice have you chosen?
What animals will be in your short story?
What does the first animal want?
How will the second animal react to this plan?
What happens in the end? Make sure this reflects the piece of advice you chose.

Unit 7 Resource 1

Before and after

Compare the little red rooster's life before and after he found the diamond button, and use your imagination to complete the table.

	Before finding the diamond button	After finding the diamond button
How did the little red rooster feel?		
How did people feel about him?		
What was he planning to do?		

Unit 7 Resource 2

Finders keepers!

Complete this mind map to plan your own short story about a found object. Should the original owner get their item back or is it a case of 'finders keepers'? Think of some reasons for both the finder and the keeper.

- Who lost the item?
- Who found the item?
- Where was the item found?
- How was the item found?

Item that was found:

- Why should the finder return it?
- Why should the finder keep it?

- What is the outcome?

Unit 8 Resource 1

Asking questions

Think about the ways people ask questions as a way of building a friendship. Compile lists of questions that the Mole and the Rat could ask to get to know one another. Refer to the text for details to help you.

Questions the Mole could ask	Questions the Rat could ask

Unit 8 Resource 2

The next adventure

Use the grid below to help you plan writing the next part of the story, in which the Mole and the Rat have an adventure in the Rat's boat.

What do the boat and the river look like? How does it feel to be in the boat?
What do the Mole and the Rat say to one another?
What problem, new character or new place could appear?
How do the animals feel about this?
How do they deal with it?
How do the Mole and the Rat return home? What do they say to each other now?

Unit 9 Resource 1

Dickon's character

Use the text and your own ideas to create a character profile of Dickon.

Picture	Name
	Age
Physical description	**Personality**
Likes	**Dislikes**

© HarperCollins*Publishers* Ltd 2017

81

Unit 9 Resource 2

A story starts

Use this sheet to plan the opening part of your own adventure story. First, create a main character who thinks he or she will miss out on the adventure until the last moment, using the extract to give you ideas.

As an extra challenge, try to make your story historical. What details could you include?

My main character	
Picture	Physical description
	Personality
Name	

The adventure	
What is the adventure?	
When would it take place, and how long would it take?	
Why might the main character miss out?	

How could you make your story historical? What clues could you give?

Now write the opening to your story!

Unit 10 Resource 1

Finding the features

Label the start of the playscript with the features below.

The character speaking	Stage directions	Character speech	The title of the play	Scene heading

'In the Rue Bel Tesoro' by Lin Coghlan

SCENE 1

(A busy train station crowded with travellers. Sasha and Omar arrive pushing an old-fashioned pram and carrying a bag stuffed with belongings.)

SASHA: Don't say anything, Omar; let me do the talking.

OMAR: (into the pram)

You've got to keep quiet, Valentine, we're in the station now.

(They approach a soldier checking documents at the entrance to the platform.)

SOLDIER: Papers?

SASHA: (handing over the papers)

We're going to meet our mother. She's waiting for us.

Unit 10 Resource 2

Costumes and setting

Think about how the play scene should look, and how you could make a stage set look realistic. Use the table below to note down costume ideas for each character, all the props needed and ideas about how the stage could look.

	Costume ideas
Sasha	
Omar	
The soldier	
Fran	

Props needed

Stage set ideas

Unit 11 Resource 1

The Vietnam War

The extract is set during the Vietnam War. Read the information below to understand more about this setting.

Where is Vietnam?

Vietnam is a country in south-east Asia, on the South China Sea. It shares a border with China.

When was the Vietnam War?

The Vietnam War was fought between 5 November 1955 and 30 April 1975.

Who was fighting?

The Vietnam War was, at heart, a civil war. This means that different parts of Vietnam were fighting each other. North Vietnam and Southern Vietnam disagreed about how the country should be run.

Each side was then joined by much bigger supporting countries, which made the war much bigger too. North Vietnam had support from China and Russia. Southern Vietnam was supported by the USA.

What was the war like for soldiers?

The jungles of Vietnam were a difficult place to fight a war. It was very difficult to find the enemy. Then, when soldiers did spot other soldiers, it was also difficult to see whether or not they were enemies.

Both sides used huge explosives, many helicopters and booby traps, and there were constant ambushes. They also used very harmful chemical gases on one another. The soldiers had to live in the very wet jungle for long periods of time, too, and were not always prepared for it. Many became very ill and died from infections, as well as from injuries. A huge number of them also suffered from shock and trauma because of what they saw, felt and had to do.

What was the war like for the Vietnamese people?

The war was everywhere, so everyone in Vietnam was surrounded by war. Soldiers were often desperate for food or shelter, and sometimes could not tell enemy soldiers apart from local people. In addition, the chemical gases the soldiers used on one another could not be prevented from reaching people's homes.

A lot of poor people's property was destroyed, and many people were killed. Like the soldiers, too, many Vietnamese people were traumatised by what they experienced.

© HarperCollins*Publishers* Ltd 2017

Unit 11 Resource 2

Character perspectives

Complete this table to help you in thinking about what the different characters in the scene were doing, saying, thinking and feeling.

	What they did	What they said	What they thought and felt
The storyteller			
Mother			
Grandmother			
The huge man			

Unit 12 Resource 1

Describing the painting

Use this table to help you to look at and describe the painting.

First make notes in the table, and then write a descriptive paragraph.

What people, animals or objects can you see in the painting?
What colours have been used in the painting? How do they make you feel?
Which things are in the background of the painting? Why do you think these details have been included?
Which things are in the foreground of the painting? Which do you think is the most important, and why?

Unit 12 Resource 2

Making comparisons

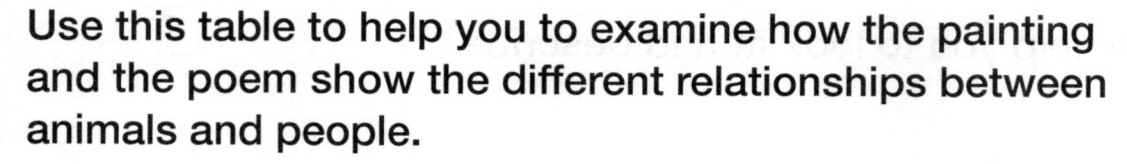

Use this table to help you to examine how the painting and the poem show the different relationships between animals and people.

First make notes in the table, and then write a descriptive paragraph.

What are the animal subjects?	
In the poem	In the painting
What are the human subjects?	
In the poem	In the painting
How do the humans feel about the animals?	
In the poem	In the painting
How do you know?	
In the poem	In the painting

Unit 13 Resource 1

Simile or metaphor?

Similes and metaphors are figures of speech. They help a writer to paint a clear picture for a reader.

Similes compare one thing to another, usually using the words 'like' or 'as'.

For example: 'My eyes sizzle like fried eggs in a pan'

What two things are being compared in this line?

The poet's _____ are being compared to

_____.

Metaphors suggest that one thing is or becomes another.

For example: 'his anger became a stormcloud'

In this line, what two things is the writer suggesting are the same?

The writer suggests that _____ really is a _____.

Now read the sentences below. At the end of each sentence, write either 'simile' or 'metaphor' to show which figure of speech appears in the sentence.

1. **From 'Angry Arthur'**

   Arthur's anger became a typhoon tipping whole towns into the sea.

2. **From 'My Hair as Black as Dirty Coal'**

   I clench my fists hard like compressing a lemon
   Until all the juice comes out.

Unit 13 Resource 2

Feeling angry

Add your ideas to this planning grid to help you think about what happens when you are angry. Then use your ideas to write your own poem or short story.

What makes you angry?	
How do you feel in the different parts of your body when you are angry?	
What things do you do when you are angry?	
What things do you say when you are angry?	
How long do you stay angry for?	
What calms you down and makes you feel better?	

Unit 14 Resource 1

True or false?

How carefully did you read the text? Check your memory by ticking true or false for each statement.

		True	False
1.	The Kori bustard can weigh up to 18 kilograms.	☐	☐
2.	The moa died out in the 1800s.	☐	☐
3.	An ostrich can run at 70 kilometres per hour.	☐	☐
4.	The bird with the longest wings is the albatross.	☐	☐
5.	Spine-tailed swifts are the fastest fliers of any living bird.	☐	☐
6.	The roc lived in Australia.	☐	☐
7.	Penguins can swim.	☐	☐
8.	Roc eggs were eight times bigger than ostrich eggs are.	☐	☐
9.	The ostrich is the biggest bird alive today.	☐	☐
10.	There is one bird smaller than a bee hummingbird.	☐	☐
11.	The Kori bustard is the heaviest bird alive that can fly.	☐	☐
12.	Ostriches can't fly.	☐	☐

Unit 14 Resource 2

Bird fact file

Make a fact file about one bird mentioned in the text. Use subheadings, diagrams and lots of facts to make your fact file interesting for a reader.

First, plan your fact file.

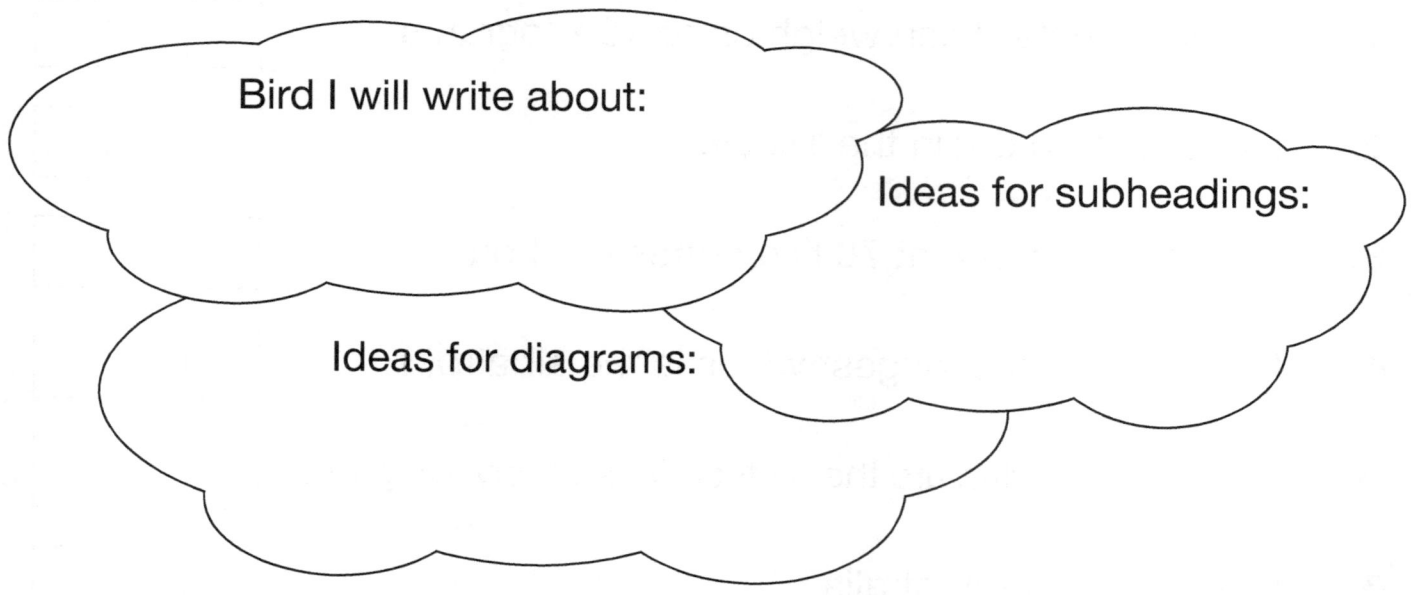

- Bird I will write about:
- Ideas for subheadings:
- Ideas for diagrams:

Now write your fact file here.

All about _____	
Section 1	Diagram 1
Section 2	Diagram 2
Section 3	

Unit 15 Resource 1

The sun

Complete this mind map to lay out different descriptions of the sun. Use the information text, the poem and your own ideas.

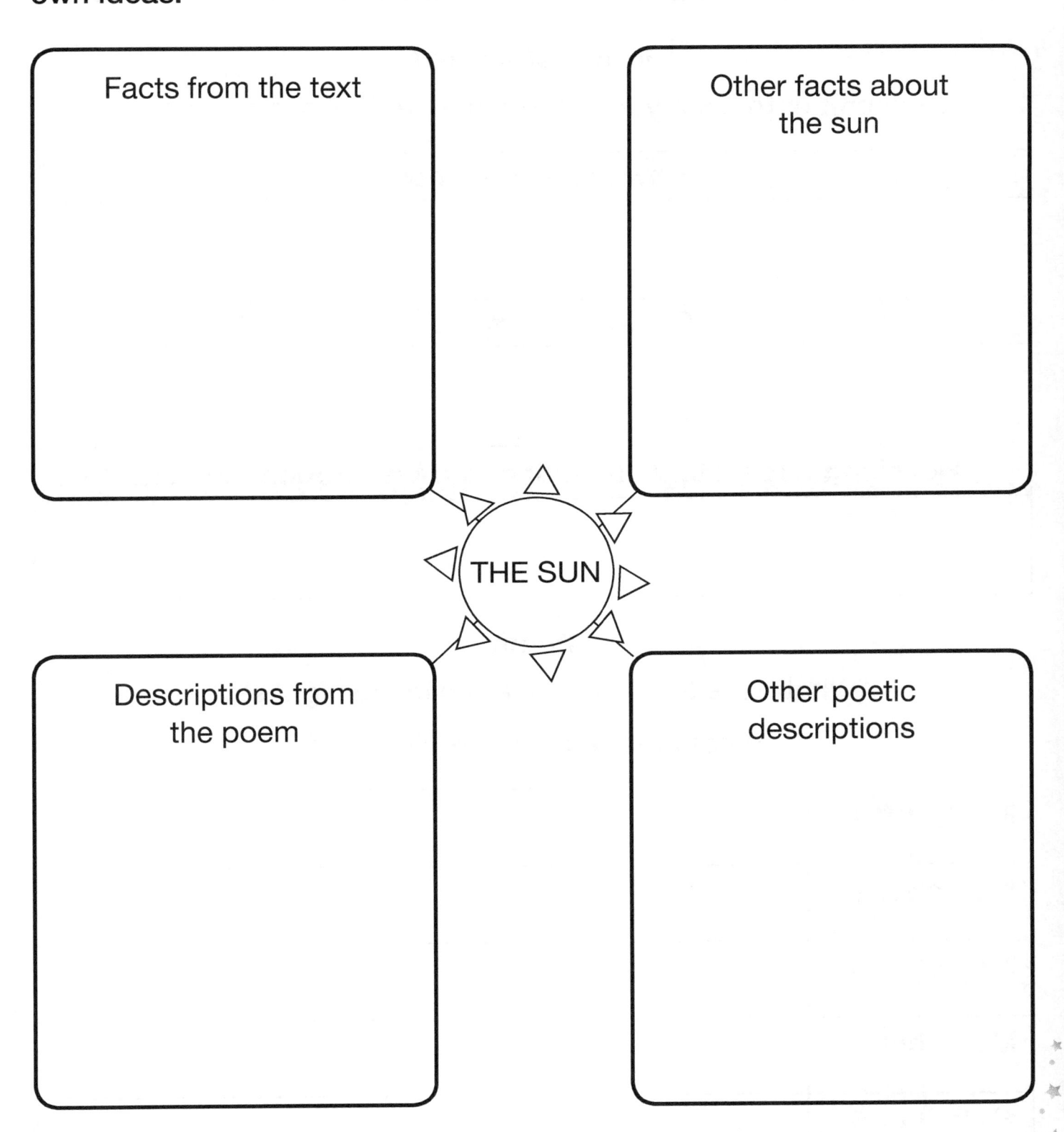

Facts from the text	Other facts about the sun

THE SUN

Descriptions from the poem	Other poetic descriptions

Unit 15 Resource 2

The moon

Write your own texts about the moon. Using the extracts for guidance, plan one information text and one poem with metaphors. Use the planning grids below and then write your texts.

Information text

(Remember to keep your information factual and accurate.)

How big is the moon?
Of what is it made up?
How long does it take the moon to travel around the earth?

Poem

(What does the moon look like in the night sky?

What other things look like this?)

Metaphor 1	
Metaphor 2	
Metaphor 3	
Metaphor 4	
Metaphor 5	

Unit 16 Resource 1

Whale fact file

Use this template and the poem to create a fact file about whales.

What do whales look like?	
What do they eat?	Where do they live?
What are they good at?	What aren't they good at?
What are the problems faced by whales?	
Why should people know about the problems whales face?	What can we do to help?

Unit 16 Resource 2

A letter to whale hunters

Write a letter to an imaginary company that sells products made from whale meat, bone and/or oil. Try to persuade them to stop what they are doing.

Ideas to think about:

- Introduce yourself and why you are writing.
- Use a polite but firm and clear tone.
- Try to make the company director feel bad about what the company is doing.
- Give at least two different reasons.
- Use a different paragraph for each reason.
- Tell the company director what you think they should do to help the whales.

Date: _____

Dear Company Director,

Yours sincerely,

_____

Unit 17 Resource 1

Now and then

Pretend you are Ruby or Tom. Write two diary entries: one about your plans before you know the gang of new children has arrived, and one about how you feel afterwards.

Before seeing the new children

After seeing the new children

Unit 17 Resource 2

Us and them

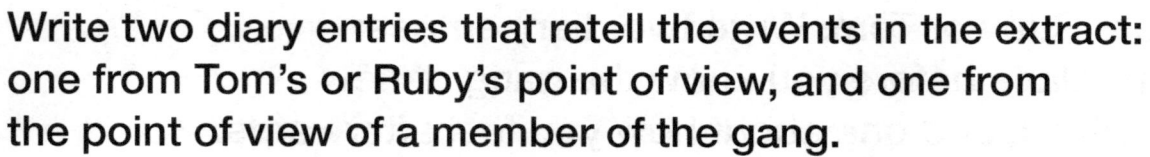

Write two diary entries that retell the events in the extract: one from Tom's or Ruby's point of view, and one from the point of view of a member of the gang.

Ruby's or Tom's diary

A gang member's diary

Unit 18 Resource 1

Sophie and Dana

Use the text and your own ideas to compare the two main characters in the scene.

How long has she been at the school?	
Sophie	Dana

Who are her friends?	
Sophie	Dana

How does she behave?	
Sophie	Dana

Why do you think she behaves like this?	
Sophie	Dana

© HarperCollins*Publishers* Ltd 2017

Unit 18 Resource 2

Different characters

Complete this table to help you in thinking about the four different characters in the scene. Look at how each of the girls acts and decide what you think this means.

Character name	
An example of something she said or did	
What you think she is like	

Character name	
An example of something she said or did	
What you think she is like	

Character name	
An example of something she said or did	
What you think she is like	

Character name	
An example of something she said or did	
What you think she is like	

Unit 19 Resource 1

True or false?

How carefully did you read the text? Check your memory by ticking true or false for each statement.

		True	False
1.	Telescopes were invented in the early 1600s.	☐	☐
2.	Galileo was an Italian scientist.	☐	☐
3.	Jupiter has rings.	☐	☐
4.	The Milky Way is made of billions of planets.	☐	☐
5.	John Michell called black holes 'dark stars'.	☐	☐
6.	He wrote about them in the 1800s.	☐	☐
7.	Dark stars are made of rock.	☐	☐
8.	In the 20th century, scientists found signs that dark stars do exist.	☐	☐
9.	A black hole isn't actually a hole.	☐	☐
10.	Spaceships can travel through back holes like they are tunnels.	☐	☐
11.	Objects that go near a black hole get pushed away.	☐	☐
12.	Black holes can swallow things as big as planets.	☐	☐

Unit 19 Resource 2

Once upon a time, in space …

Use the information you have learned to write a short story about a team of astronauts who come across a black hole while on a space mission.

Answer the questions in the planning grid before you start to write your story.

Who is in the astronaut team?

What is the original mission?

How does the team discover the black hole?

What problem does the black hole present?

What do the team do about it?

How does the story end?

Unit 20 Resource 1

Tiger's plan

Imagine you are Tiger. Make notes about your plan.

MY PLAN!

Overall aim:

Who will be involved:

How I will get animals to my house:

How I will get each animal on its own:

What my wife will do and say:

What I will do then:

Unit 20 Resource 2

Anansi's plan

Imagine you are Anansi, and have just overheard Tiger. Make notes about what you plan to do to stop him.

- What have I overheard?
- What do I think about it?
- What do I want to do about it?
- How will I achieve this?
- What do I think will happen to Tiger in the end?